"Honest. Meaty. In your face. *Standing Firm* is all of that and more, and believe me it's all good. Donna Partow echoes my own spirit in this soul-searching study that challenges us to answer some deep questions about where we really live. Donna tackles the issue of standing no matter what life brings your way by applying biblical truths to the reality of living that will give you the second wind you need in order to continue this journey. This is one that I will be giving to friends."

Michelle McKinney Hammond
Author of *Get a Love Life,*
What to Do Until Love Finds You, and
What Becomes of the Broken Hearted

"A powerfully timely Bible study that will challenge us out of our comfort zones while providing help and healing for those with a past—which includes just about all of us."

Ellie Kay
Author of *Shop, Save, and Share* and
How to Save Money Every Day

A TEN-WEEK JOURNEY TO

Standing Firm

Donna Partow

BETHANY HOUSE
Minneapolis, Minnesota

Published by Bethany House Publishers
A Ministry of Bethany Fellowship International
11400 Hampshire Avenue South
Bloomington, Minnesota 55438
www.bethanyhouse.com

Printed in the United States of America by
Bethany Press International, Bloomington, Minnesota 55438

Library of Congress Cataloging-in-Publication Data

Partow, Donna.
  Ten-week journey to standing firm / Donna Partow.
     p. cm.
  ISBN 0-7642-2293-7
  1. Christian women—Religious life. 2. Christian life—Biblical teaching.
3. Determination (Personality trait)—Biblical teaching. I. Title.
  BV4527 .P378   2001
  248.8′43—dc21
                                    2001002455

To Deborah Lovett,
who gave me the courage to Stand Firm

Therefore, thus says the Lord,
If you return, then I will restore you—
Before Me you will stand;
And if you extract the precious from the worthless
You will become My spokesman.

Jeremiah 15:19 (NASB)

Bethany House Books
by Donna Partow

Becoming a Vessel God Can Use
Living in Absolute Freedom
Standing Firm
Walking in Total God-Confidence
A Woman's Guide to Personality Types

DONNA PARTOW is a Christian communicator with a compelling testimony of God's transforming power. From her childhood as "the kid no one was allowed to play with" to her days as a drug dealer and her marriage to a strict Middle Eastern husband, she shares her life journey with disarming honesty and humor.

Donna's uncommon transparency and passion for Christ have been used by God at women's conferences and retreats around the country. She has been a popular guest on more than one hundred radio and TV programs, including *Focus on the Family*.

She is the bestselling author of numerous books including *Becoming a Vessel God Can Use*.

If your church sponsors an annual women's retreat, perhaps they would be interested in learning more about Donna's special weekend program. For more information, contact:

Donna Partow
P.O. Box 842
Payson, AZ 85541
(520) 472–7368
e-mail: donnapartow@cybertrails.com

Contents

WEEK ONE:
Seek God First

This Week's Verse:

But without faith it is impossible to please Him, for he who
comes to God must believe that He is, and that He is a
rewarder of those who diligently seek Him.

Hebrews 11:6 (NKJV)

Day One

Fluorescent Pink T-shirts

But without faith it is impossible to please Him, for he who comes to God must believe that He is, and that He is a rewarder of those who diligently seek Him.

Hebrews 11:6 (NKJV)

I want you to imagine that you're standing in a crowded room, wearing a fluorescent pink T-shirt. I want you to imagine that your five-year-old daughter made it for you as a Mother's Day gift by dipping her hands in silver glitter and pressing them firmly upon the front of the shirt. She then took fabric paint and scrawled her autograph below the handprints. This T-shirt is one of a kind. It may not be fashionable, it may not be elegant, but it's yours. And there will never be another quite like it, anywhere in the world. You wouldn't dream of trading it in, even if you could.

Now I want you to imagine your sister walking up to you and saying, "I can't believe you are wearing that ridiculous black thing. It's completely inappropriate."

You point out to her, "It's pink. And what's so inappropriate about a T-shirt?"

Your sister shakes her head in frustration and snaps, "Whatever you say," as she storms off. You're left scratching your head, puzzled. You walk over to your mom and mention your sister's unusual comment. Your mom also gets upset. "Your sister is trying to help you. Maybe you should listen for once in your life." And she storms off, too. Now you're seriously confused.

Then a neighbor waves to you from across the room. What a relief! It's good to see someone normal, unlike your off-the-wall family. But when you approach, she doesn't seem pleased. She addresses you harshly, "I can't believe you came out in public dressed like that. You're making a spectacle of yourself, walking around in a bikini top. I'm extremely disappointed in you."

"But it's not a bikini. Look at it. It's just a T-shirt. It's a fluorescent pink T-shirt. My daughter made it for me." As you desperately try to explain yourself, your pastor walks over and solemnly declares, "I hope you realize that you have destroyed your testimony for Christ."

For a moment, you begin to wonder if they're right. Maybe you're *not* wearing a pink T-shirt with your daughter's handprints on the front. Maybe you're wearing a black bikini top. You run to the bathroom and stare in the mirror. No doubt about it. It's a pink fluorescent T-shirt.

You return to the room, only to find that a large crowd has gathered, all of them expressing their shock and outrage over your black bikini.

How would you respond?

Would you argue with them?

Would you walk out?

Would they be able to convince you to surrender what you knew to be true?

Or could you stand firm in their midst, quietly confident of the truth?

This is a book about fluorescent pink T-shirts. It's about having the courage to believe the truth, even when everyone around you says you are wrong. It's about proudly wearing the unique T-shirt God has given you, the one with his handprints and his signature scrawled across the front. It's about declaring with quiet confidence: "This is the T-shirt I'm wearing because this is the T-shirt God custom-made for me. It may not be fashionable. It may not be elegant. But it's mine. God gave it to me. And I wouldn't trade it for anything in the world."

It's about living the life God has handed you, without explanation, without apology.

It's about *Standing Firm.*

These are the lessons God has spent the last year teaching me. They are the lessons I'd like to share with you over the coming weeks. This book is the fourth in a series of "ten-week journeys" I have written. The others were *Becoming A Vessel God Can Use, Walking in Total God-Confidence,* and *Living in Absolute Freedom.* People often ask if they have to do the studies in the order I wrote them. Not necessarily. If you've picked up this book without having read the others, I'm confident you will benefit by it. But I do believe those of you who have traveled through some of the previous books will find it particularly meaningful.

I've been deeply touched by the thousands of e-mails and letters I have received from all over the world in response to my previous writing. Many people wrote that when they finished my last book, they cried, because they felt like they were saying good-bye to an old friend. Well, in writing this latest book, I honestly feel like I'm saying "hello again" to my old friends.

Many readers have observed that I write from a broken heart, and that God uses my brokenness to heal the brokenhearted. Never has that been more true than on the pages of this book. I think you will find this to be my most personal, my most passionate writing to date. As you turn the pages, I hope you'll laugh; I know you'll cry. My prayer is that through it all, you'll grow closer to the heart of God.

The other frequent comment I hear, and this one blows me away, is that God speaks to people very personally, very directly, through my books. When they read each day's lesson, they don't hear *me*, they hear God. I can't imagine why the God of the universe would choose to work through my writing in such a way. It's certainly not because of my literary brilliance or the profundity of my stories. You'll find that my writing style is very down-to-earth; my stories are simple tales from my everyday life. Most of the lessons I share were learned the hard way: by falling down. I'm only learning how to stand firm after having mastered the art of stumbling.

Along the way, I've realized that discovering a new truth is one thing; working that truth into your daily life is quite another. Discovery doesn't automatically lead to transformation. You can read a hundred books, but if you don't *apply* what you are supposedly learning, what's the point? I assume you've decided to tackle this study because you long for transformation. I've got good news. This *can* be an absolutely life-changing experience for you. Or it can be just another book sitting on your shelf. The choice is yours.

Let's assume you choose the life-changing path. What will that involve? First, you must do more than read the book; you must prayerfully *work through* it. That means taking it slow, one day at a time, thoughtfully answering every question. It means reading with a high-lighter in your hand, memorizing the Scripture verses, and frequently reviewing the key points from each week. (To make this easier, you'll find perforated cards with the verses and key points in the back of the book. Carry them with you wherever you go.) Also, take time each week to complete the Weekly Review.

Second, share the truths you are learning. The simplest way to do this is to join others who are on the same journey, so you can gather once a week to discuss the lesson. This can be done as a weekly women's Bible study, or you can get together with a friend or two. I've heard from many people who are doing it via the Internet and still others who are doing it as a husband-wife or mother-daughter team. I just hung up the phone from talking with a sixty-three-year-old Indiana woman who is leading her daughter and two daughters-in-law through *Living in Absolute Freedom*. They've done all three studies and have pledged to tackle this one as soon as it comes out! Even if you are not working through the study with someone, you can share the truths during informal conversation with family and friends.

Finally, make a firm commitment to stay the course, to stand firm until the end. My prayer is that by the time you've completed the study, you will be able to say, as you reflect upon the life you've lived and consider the road ahead, *"This is the journey I am on . . . because this is the journey I am on."*

It may not be the journey you would have chosen for yourself, but because it is the journey God has chosen for you, you will embrace it.

At the heart of that embrace is a determination to seek God first. Recently, I was speaking at a conference alongside of singer-song-writer Jamie Owens-Collins, perhaps best known for penning "The Battle Belongs to the Lord." Jamie shared a word in due season when she pointed out Hebrews 11:6, noting that God IS a rewarder of those who diligently seek him. It's who he IS. It's not just something he does. And sometimes he doesn't do. It is his very nature to be a re-warder of those who diligently seek him. He cannot NOT reward a diligent seeker. The reward may not be a new car! Or even a perfect life. But as the Lord pointed out to Abraham after he had survived a very tough battle, "I am your shield, your very great reward" (Genesis 15:1).

That's why I am absolutely confident that God will reward your efforts as you diligently seek him through the pages of this book. So stay the course. Stand firm. God will reward you for it.

Stand at the Crossroads and Look:

1. What has motivated you to begin this journey?

2. Express your hopes for the upcoming ten-week journey. Describe where you want to be—emotionally, spiritually, relationally, and physically—ten weeks from now. What changes do you hope to see in your life by the time you've completed *Standing Firm*?

3. Write out a prayer committing yourself to finish what you've started.

4. What key lesson did you glean from today's study?

Truths to Stand Upon:

- Standing firm means believing the truth, even when no one else around you does.
- Standing firm means living the life God has handed you, without explanation, without apology.
- We often learn how to stand firm only after mastering the art of stumbling.

Day Two

A Place to Stand

When the storm has swept by, the wicked are gone,
but the righteous stand firm forever.

Proverbs 10:25

I love the ocean. One glimpse of the waves pounding the beach and my mind is filled with remembrances of days spent on the beaches of New Jersey in my girlhood. Of my brothers building sand castles and my sisters working on their suntans. Of my father's boat sailing off into the early morning sun and later hauling in a load of flounder and bluefish before sunset. Of greedy seagulls plummeting down to grab a bite of someone's leftover sandwich. The smell of the salt air and the feel of sand everywhere. Then as night fell, the sound of the boardwalk hawkers as we wandered from pier to pier in search of excitement

And the hope that life would always be so magical.

Yet it wasn't always magical. I remember storms, too. Raging. Frightening. Unpredictable. Storms that appeared out of the clear blue sky, spoiling our plans. Even after the storm subsided, the surf would remain rough. That's a very dangerous fact of life. But as a child, this was cause for jubilation; it meant bigger waves.

Late one afternoon, my brother and I were frolicking amid such storm-swept wonders when it happened. From below, I was trapped by a powerful undercurrent, determined to drag me out to sea. From above, I was buffeted by waves tossing me back toward the beach. My body rolled over and over and over, as the two forces of nature battled for dominion.

For what seemed like a breathless eternity, I struggled for life. Struggled to find a place where I could stand firm. When I finally broke free and took my stand, I discovered I had been tossing around in three feet of water.

Have you ever felt overpowered by forces outside of your control? Have you ever felt like you were being pulled by undercurrents and pushed by the waves of life? Perhaps this past year, you've faced circumstances that overwhelmed you and left you struggling just to keep two feet firmly planted on the ground.

If so, you're not alone. That's the kind of year I've just lived through. Although I'm shaken, just like I was that late afternoon on the beach, I believe my feet are now firmly planted on solid ground. And the water is not nearly as deep as I had imagined it to be. Rough to be sure. But certainly not so deep that the love of God is not deeper still. We need only seek him. He is there.

He is there and ready to rescue. Just a few hours ago, I was searching frantically for a computer CD which I needed to have in order to finish this book on time. (I only have three days until my deadline, but don't worry, the rest of the book is already written. I save the first and last weeks for last!) Anyway, I had worked myself into an absolute frenzy, running around the house ripping apart drawers, throwing files in the air. I was crawling around on my office floor, amidst stacks and stacks of scattered paper (at this point, there's not even a *path* anymore), ready to burst into tears. Suddenly I stopped, stood up, and said out loud, "Father, you know where that CD is. It's in this house. Show me where." Within seconds, I knew the answer. I calmly walked downstairs, opened junk drawer #289, and there it was.

A little thing?

I guess so, but I'll also tell you this. Over these past months, as I have faced the most difficult trial of my life, God has met me at every single turn. Every time I felt myself being swept away by waves of pain, God was there. God was there and no matter how cliché it may sound, I must tell you the plain truth: The only place I ever found to stand was upon his Word. Every answer he spoke to my heart was drawn from Scriptures I had already known. Some of them I didn't even know I knew. But they were down there somewhere, tucked away in my heart, and the Spirit of God was able to bring them to my remembrance, guide me to them, or just let me stumble upon them exactly—exactly—when I needed them most.

Let me give you an example. As 2001 began, I was reflecting back, trying to make sense of it all, wondering what on earth had happened to my life. On January 8, during my morning Bible reading, I found a place to stand. God clearly spoke to my heart and said, "This is what the past year was all about. Read, my child, and understand."

Psalm 124:2–8

If the Lord had not been on our side
  when men attacked us,
when their anger flared against us,
  they would have swallowed us alive;
the flood would have engulfed us,
  the torrent would have swept over us,
the raging waters
  would have swept us away.
Praise be to the Lord,
  who has not let us be torn by their teeth.
We have escaped like a bird
  out of the fowler's snare;
the snare has been broken,
  and we have escaped.
Our help is in the name of the Lord,
  the Maker of heaven and earth.

Okay, so only the first stanza ties in with our "wave" theme for the day, but it's all so good I couldn't resist sharing it. Let's face it. If the Lord is not on your side, you WILL be swallowed alive. You will be engulfed and swept away by the raging waters of life. That's why it's so vitally important for us to seek God first. Not as a last resort. Not when we've run out of other ideas. First. God doesn't say the waves won't come. But he DOES say we don't have to let them overtake us. Sometimes we let the world toss us around far longer than we have to, we struggle longer than we should, all because we refuse to seek God. Help is there! Our help is in the name of the Lord! If you can't quite stand yet, just scream for help the next time you come up for air. *The* Lifeguard promises to come running to your rescue.

Stand at the Crossroads and Look:

1. Have you ever felt buffeted by forces that were outside of your control? Are you facing such a situation right now? Describe.

2. Have you ever had a situation like my search for the CD? Have you ever been in turmoil, but when you finally stopped and called out to God, he provided the answer you needed?

3. Are you inclined to seek God first? Or turn to him as a last resort?

4. Write out a prayer asking God to enable you to stand firm in the face of life's storms.

5. What key lesson did you glean from today's study?

Truths to Stand Upon:

- Sometimes we are overwhelmed by forces outside of our control.
- If you can't quite stand yet, just scream for help the next time you come up for air. *The* Lifeguard promises to come running to your rescue.

Day Three

Stand and Look

This is what the Lord says:
"Stand at the crossroads and look;
ask for the ancient paths,
ask where the good way is, and walk in it,
and you will find rest for your souls.
But you said, 'We will not walk in it.' "

Jeremiah 6:16

When we moved to our homestead in the mountains a couple years ago, we brought with us two very stupid dogs, whom I've dubbed Stinker and Dinker. I occasionally go so low as to call them Dumb and Dumber. Although we have two acres of land and are surrounded by an additional twenty-plus acres of uninhabited land, our dogs like to run out into the road. Now, if I were a dog, I'd like to run around the woods chasing rabbits and quail. Well, apparently these dogs just don't think like I do. They prefer standing in the road. And since they are exceedingly dumb, it hasn't occurred to them that they should get out of the road when a car drives by.

Apparently, our dogs creating a dirt-road version of a traffic jam did not amuse some of our neighbors. They kidnapped our dogs and turned them over to the authorities. Being dutiful pet owners, we marched down to the pound and promptly bailed them out to the tune of $200.

We put them on chains, but they kept breaking loose. A few more kidnapping (followed by bailing-out) episodes later, and we knew we needed to try something else. I guess we're not that quick to catch on ourselves, because by the time we came to the dramatic conclusion that what we were doing wasn't working, we had donated a small fortune to the local dogcatcher.

We spent another couple hundred bucks buying a dog run (for the uninitiated, that's a three-foot-by-eight-foot cage). The heartbroken dogs barked day and night. I wonder if they ever realized that it was their own folly that ruined their freedom?

God has given us a great big beautiful world to roam about in. He filled it with forests, rivers, oceans, and countless other wonderful things to behold. He created our fellow human beings for us to love and serve. He gave us families, friends, and good causes to devote our time to. He left us with a Great Commission and invites us to join him in ministering healing to a hurting world. We live in a world filled with wonderful places to go and valuable ways to invest our time.

So why do we insist on running out in the middle of the road? Why do we go to the most dangerous place around? Why do we waste so much of our lives standing around looking—and acting—stupid? Let's face it. Sometimes we're dumb and sometimes we're even dumber.

God has given us great freedom,[1] but we often choose to squander it. Then when we find ourselves in cages of our own creation, we bark at our circumstances and the people around us. In our search for someone to blame, we even bark at God. We fail to realize that our own folly ruins our freedom.

God wants to open your cage door. He wants you to embrace your liberty and see what wonderful things can come of it. It grieves him to see you standing in the middle of the road, putting your life in jeopardy. It breaks his heart to keep bailing you out of your latest disaster.

There IS a better way to live.

> This is what the Lord says:
> "Stand at the crossroads and look;
>   ask for the ancient paths,
> ask where the good way is, and walk in it,
>   and you will find rest for your souls." (Jeremiah 6:16)

Will you stand at the crossroads of your life today and look? Will you be honest with yourself about where you are and how you got there? Will you be humble enough to seek God, asking him to show

---

[1]For more on this topic, please see my previous book *Living in Absolute Freedom*.

you another way to live? And when God shows you the good way, will you determine to walk in it? If so, God offers you a promise instead of a cage. You will find rest for your soul. And wouldn't you really rather rest than run anyway?

Stand at the Crossroads and Look:

1. In what ways have you chosen to "run out in the middle of the road"?

2. What have been the consequences of that choice?

3. Can you think of a time when you found yourself in a "cage of your own creation"? Describe.

4. Have you been barking at your circumstances? At the people around you? At God?

5. Write out a prayer asking God to rescue you from "standing out in the middle of the road looking stupid" or to release you from the "cage of your own creation."

6. What key lesson did you glean from today's study?

Truths to Stand Upon:

- We become "caged in" by our own foolish choices, but God wants us to regain our freedom.
- To live well, we must stand and look honestly at our lives.

Day Four

Things Above

Since, then, you have been raised with Christ, set your hearts on things above, where Christ is seated at the right hand of God. Set your minds on things above, not on earthly things.

Colossians 3:1–2

Isn't it weird how the same thing can have such different effects on different people? Running is a case in point. Running can give one man a heart attack, while enabling another man to stay fit for life. For one man, it's a matter of life. For the other, a matter of death. What's the difference? With few exceptions, the difference is practice. The difference is focus.

The man who dies from running—the one whose heart is overwhelmed—probably hasn't been working his heart. He hasn't been focused on strengthening it day by day, little by little. Instead, he's been neglecting it. Then when he most needs his heart to do its job—to function the way God designed it to—it fails him.

The man who derives life and health from running has been paying his dues over a long period of time. One day, he took a walk around the block. He was out of breath. His heart registered a protest. But he did the same thing the very next day. And the day after that. And pretty soon his heart got with the program. It began to respond. To grow strong. To perform as it should. Some months later, he livened his step into a light jog and maintained the pace for a few blocks. Gradually, his heart grew even stronger. It didn't happen overnight, but it did happen.

All the good intentions in the world can't strengthen your heart. I learned this firsthand when my father had a heart attack on New Year's Eve, 1996. I was living in Arizona and he was on the East

Coast. The moment I hung up the phone after learning the news, I threw a few items into a carry-on bag and went flying out the door on the way to the airport. Upon arriving, I discovered there was a plane leaving in ten minutes—it was the last flight of the evening. If I ran flat-out, I could make it.

I had never been more determined to run in my entire life. Every fiber of my being *wanted* to run. But my heart failed me. I just *couldn't keep running*. I hadn't practiced. I hadn't prepared. I had always assumed that adrenaline would be enough to get anyone through those types of situations. It's not true. When the critical moment came, I was simply unprepared to endure. When I arrived at the gate, the door was closed, and the plane was heading toward the runway.

Just as we neglect our physical, literal heart, we neglect our spiritual heart as well. We like to tell ourselves that we can get away with such neglect. That, somehow, when we need to rise to the occasion, we'll have enough spiritual adrenaline to see us through. I don't think that's the case.

Those who are able to stand firm in the midst of a crisis are those who consciously work to strengthen their heart. And how do we do that? By seeking God first. By deliberately choosing to set our hearts (and minds) on things above.

Wanting is not the same as choosing. Wanting is a feeling; choosing is an act of the will.

I know you are moving beyond feeling to choosing because you have chosen to read this book. Maybe today is the first day in *years* that you have gone for a "spiritual walk around the block." Or maybe it's just part of your ordinary "jogging routine." Either way, your heart will grow stronger every day as you make a determined effort to lead a healthier lifestyle—a lifestyle that includes a daily workout for your spiritual heart!

Let's say you're out of shape. Maybe you've even had a heart attack and are teetering on the edge of spiritual death. I have some great news for you. You can be alive again. You can get well. You can stand firm. People *can* recover from a heart attack. My father did. And I was able to convince the gate agent to convince the pilot to turn the plane around and let me on. Thank God for his mercy. But let's not presume upon it.

Get beyond wanting. Start choosing.

Stand at the Crossroads and Look:

1. What's the condition of your heart? Could you survive a sprint? A marathon? Maybe you're not sure you could make it around the block!

2. Can you think of a time when you were counting on "spiritual adrenaline" to get you through? Did it work?

3. Write out a prayer asking God to strengthen you as you seek to strengthen your heart.

4. What key lesson did you glean from today's study?

Truths to Stand Upon:

- We can't count on spiritual adrenaline to get us through the crises of life.
- We need to strengthen our spiritual hearts through daily exercise.

Day Five

He Will Guide You

The Lord will guide you always;
he will satisfy your needs in a sun-scorched land
and will strengthen your frame.
You will be like a well-watered garden,
like a spring whose waters never fail.
Your people will rebuild the ancient ruins
and will raise up the age-old foundations;
you will be called Repairer of Broken Walls,
Restorer of Streets with Dwellings.

Isaiah 58:11–12

I live in Arizona, so I know about sun-scorched land, about desert places inhabited only by rattlesnakes and Gila monsters. In the desert, there are no landmarks to guide you. Everything looks the same. A cactus is a cactus. You could go in circles for miles and never know it. Then again, you could be making tremendous progress, even though it feels like you're going in circles. Yet God has said he will satisfy our needs, even in desert places.

I wish I could tell you that every day of your spiritual journey will be like a day at the beach. Not the kind where you get swept away by waves, but the kind where you kick back and take it easy. I wish I could tell you that every day for the next ten weeks, you'll leap out of bed, eager to spend quiet time with the Lord, your Bible in one hand and this book in the other. To be honest, I have heard from many people who have had that experience. However, I suspect that most of you, at some point along your journey through this book, will go through a sun-scorched place. A place where it feels like no spiritual progress is being made. That's when you'll have to make a choice. Will you allow God to guide you forward? Or will you turn back?

Anyone can follow God when the following is easy, but God offers a promise to those of us who will continue following even when it's tough. God says he will strengthen you and make you like a well-watered garden. In other words, he'll give you what you need to grow. Yet he goes one further. Not only will you experience personal growth, but God will also enable you to make a difference in the lives of others. You will rebuild ancient ruins—repairing the fallout of problems that may have plagued your family for generations. You'll provide a new, solid foundation for your children to build upon after you. God will even enable you to make a difference in your community as you become a "repairer of broken walls" and the "restorer of streets." That means you'll be an agent of security and peace, a haven of rest for the weary. As you stand firm, you'll discover that people will come to you in their time of crisis. You, in turn, can point them to the only One who can guide them through a sun-scorched land.

This week, we examined the importance of Seeking God First. In the coming weeks, we'll cover nine additional attitudes and actions that enable a person to stand firm. To stand firm, you must also:

Sustain God's Perspective
Satisfy Your Spiritual Hunger
Savor the Love God Has for You
Strengthen Yourself Against the Attacks of the Enemy
Speak Truth to Yourself and Others
Stem the Tide of Mediocrity
Suffer Like a Saint
Serve Wholeheartedly
Stand Firm Until the End

Ten key words I want you to remember: Seek. Sustain. Satisfy. Savor. Strengthen. Speak. Stem. Suffer. Serve. Stand. May God bless you and keep you in the coming days and weeks as you seek to incorporate these actions and attitudes into your daily life.

Stand at the Crossroads and Look:

1. What will you do if you encounter a sun-scorched place along this journey?

2. What promise does God offer to those who stand firm when they'd rather give up?

3. Write out a prayer asking God to guide you always.

4. What key lesson did you glean from today's study?

5. Write out This Week's Verse from memory.

Truths to Stand Upon:

- God has promised to guide us always, even through a sun-scorched land.
- Ten key words to remember: Seek. Sustain. Satisfy. Savor. Strengthen. Speak. Stem. Suffer. Serve. Stand.

Weekly Review

Take a few moments to fill in the ten actions and attitudes required to Stand Firm. Don't worry—this exercise will get easier as the weeks progress. For now, look in the back of the book if you need help.

S _____ God first

S _____ God's perspective

S _____ your spiritual hunger

S _____ the love God has for you

S _____ yourself against the attacks of the enemy

S _____ truth to yourself and others

S _____ the tide of mediocrity

S _____ like a saint

S _____ wholeheartedly

S _____ firm until the end

WEEK TWO:
Sustain God's Perspective

This Week's Verse:

Call to me and I will answer you and tell you great and
unsearchable things that you do not know.

Jeremiah 33:3

Day One

God's Phone Number

Call to me and I will answer you and tell you great and unsearchable things you do not know.

Jeremiah 33:3

Do you know your phone number? Dumb question, right? Do you know your best friend's phone number? Even dumber question! Okay, here's one for you: Are there phone numbers your *fingers* know even though *you* don't? My fingers know my best friend's phone number. They could dial it this very second. But I honestly couldn't tell you what it is . . . unless I watched my fingers in action. Do you know what I mean?

How about God's phone number? Do you know that one? Have you dialed it so many times that your fingers could dial it for you? His phone number is Jeremiah 33:3. "Call to me and I WILL answer you" (emphasis added). No answering machines in heaven, thank God! And the best part is this. When we call him, he will tell us "great and unsearchable things" that we don't know. When was the last time you called someone who was able to tell you "great and unsearchable things" you didn't know? Now, they may have been able to feed you a morsel or two of new gossip, so that would qualify as "things you do not know." But great? I don't think so.

I often quip that when we face a crisis in our lives, we can either take it to the phone or take it to the throne. Guess I need to revise that. We *can* take it to the phone, as long as it's the phone that goes straight to the throne.

I am all in favor of seeking counsel from our friends and family. In fact, I think we must. The Scripture says "there is wisdom in the counsel of many." However, if we want to sustain God's perspective, then we better sustain a conversation with God himself.

Think about this for a minute. If you want to get Diane's perspective on something, would you call Sharon? Sharon may know Diane extremely well. She may be her walking partner every morning. She'll probably have some great insight about what Diane might think or believe. She might be able to shed some light on Diane's perspective. You could then go talk to a bunch of Diane's other friends—all people who know her well and have a good sense of how she thinks and feels. You could spend weeks on this little endeavor. All these conversations might prove enlightening, but it seems to me that if you really want to get Diane's perspective, you should just ask *her*. Wouldn't that be a whole lot easier?

Here's what I try to do when I'm at a crossroads in my life. I seek God first (Week One). I try to grab hold of and sustain God's perspective. Once I have done that, however, I ask God to confirm what I believe he has said. It has been my experience that God *always* confirms his message. In fact, the surest way to test whether or not you've truly gotten God's perspective on something is to watch for confirmation.

His confirmation may come from a variety of sources: A song. A sermon. A radio broadcast. A phone conversation with a friend. Maybe even an e-mail.

I had been thinking about this passage, when out of the clear blue I received an e-mail from Brenda Huser, a women's ministry director in Wichita, Kansas. Brenda and I worked closely together when I spoke at her women's retreat last year. We hit it off and have kept in touch ever since. Here's what Brenda had to say:

> God showed me a verse the other day that I wanted to share with you: Jeremiah 33:3: "Call to me and I will answer you and tell you great and unsearchable things you do not know." In my NIV Study Bible notes it says: "As the rest of chapter 33 demonstrates, the Lord will first judge his people and then restore them in ways that will be nothing short of incredible." The title of Chapter 33 is "Promise of Restoration." God was speaking to me about Hope as a church. I believe that he used the retreat when you spoke in this process. God used you to bring his message.

So God used me to take his message to their church, then he used Brenda to send a message to me! Yes, God speaks through his people. Get ready for this. The very next day at Bible study, our teacher said our new memory verse for the coming week was . . . Can you guess? Jeremiah 33:3.

You probably think I make this stuff up! But I don't. Believe me, when God wants to get a message to us, he does so clearly. There can be no mistake about it. God isn't playing games with us. He doesn't have one of those answering machines with garbled messages. And when he leaves a message on our machine, he doesn't talk so fast that we can't catch what he's saying. (One of my all-time pet peeves is when people say their phone number so quickly, you'd think they were running a marathon!)

God *wants* us to call upon him. He will never treat us the way we treat telemarketers who call during the dinner hour. He will never treat us like we are interrupting him. He *wants* to tell us great and unsearchable things. He *wants* us to hear what he is saying. God is even more eager for us to sustain his perspective than we are to grab hold of it.

So call him! He promises to answer.

Stand at the Crossroads and Look:

1. Where do you run in a crisis? To the phone or to the throne?

2. Do you rely too heavily on *other* people to tell you God's perspective, rather than going directly to God?

3. Who are the people you've been relying on? List them. They may be great friends of God, but so are you! Pray about each name, and ask God to show you if it's possible that you have been putting them in the place of God.

4. Write out a prayer calling upon God and asking him a specific question you need to get his perspective on.

5. What key lesson did you glean from today's study?

Truths to Stand Upon:

- When we call upon God, he will answer us.
- If we want God's perspective, we should ask God.

Day Two

God's Plans

"For I know the plans I have for you," declares the Lord, "plans to prosper you and not to harm you, plans to give you hope and a future."

Jeremiah 29:11

I've noticed that at various crossroads in my life, when people want to share an encouraging Scripture, they frequently quote Jeremiah 29:11. Typically, when I hear the same verse repeatedly, I consider it confirmation. (That's what we talked about yesterday, remember?) But occasionally, I think something else is going on. At the risk of sounding judgmental, sometimes I think we quote an oft-quoted verse because we feel like we should quote a verse and we don't know any others.

Does that sound harsh? I pray not. My only purpose is to speak the truth in love. I believe there are certain passages that are overworked because we are not spending enough time memorizing *other* passages. I believe Jeremiah 29:11 is such a passage.

Now, don't get me wrong. I love that passage, too. It is one of my favorites. I have quoted it myself many times. However, the danger with familiar passages is that we often take them out of context. Let's look at the context of this verse, the book of Jeremiah. We'll pick up where we left off yesterday:

" 'Call to me and I will answer you and tell you great and unsearchable things you do not know.' For this is what the Lord, the God of Israel, says about the houses in this city and the royal palaces of Judah that have been torn down to be used against the siege ramps and the sword in the fight with the Babylonians: 'They will be filled with the dead bodies of the men I will slay in my anger and wrath. I will hide my face from this city because of all its wickedness.' " (Jeremiah 33:3–5)

Whoa! Yesterday, when we talked about calling on God and hearing great and unsearchable things, is this what you had in mind? Dead bodies everywhere? Could you possibly have predicted that the *very next verse* would be so harsh? Or would you have predicted something nice and polite like, "Call upon me and I will tell you great and unsearchable things you do not know about the brand-new house I'm gonna give you in the suburbs and that promotion I'm gonna arrange at the office."

I guess we didn't really have God's perspective after all, huh?

When you quote Jeremiah 29:11, do you ever stop to think, "What were the plans God had for *Jeremiah's* future?" Dead bodies strewn everywhere. And a life so filled with heartbreak that, to this day, Jeremiah is known as the Weeping Prophet. Scary, isn't it? Maybe it would help us to sustain God's perspective if we re-titled the verse Weeping Prophet 29:11.

So far all we know is that God's plans for Jeremiah's future included some pretty crummy stuff. But there is good news on the way. Let's go back to the "call upon me" passage and pick it up in verse 6:

> " 'Nevertheless, I will bring health and healing to it; I will heal my people and will let them enjoy abundant peace and security. I will bring Judah and Israel back from captivity and will rebuild them as they were before. I will cleanse them from all the sin they have committed against me and will forgive all their sins of rebellion against me. Then this city will bring me renown, joy, praise and honor before all nations on earth that hear of all the good things I do for it; and they will be in awe and will tremble at the abundant prosperity and peace I provide for it. . . . I will restore their fortunes and have compassion on them.' " (Jeremiah 33:6–9, 26)

Now *that's* what we had in mind when we talked about "great and unsearchable things" and "plans to prosper and not to harm." Unfortunately, this part of the prophecy wasn't fulfilled until after Jeremiah's death.

So did God lie? He promised Jeremiah a hope and a future but let him endure nightmarish circumstances. What gives? I could tell you *my* perspective. When we get to heaven, we could even ask Jeremiah for *his* perspective. For now, let's seek God's perspective. He gives it to us in Weeping Prophet 29:12–13: "Then you will call upon me and come and pray to me, and I will listen to you. You will seek me and find me when you seek me with all your heart."

It comes back to the phone call, doesn't it? It turns out that the "great and unsearchable" answer isn't really the point. The *phone call* is the point. The relationship is the point. God is not nearly as concerned about the condition of our circumstances as he is about the condition of our heart. From God's point of view, a great future is one in which we sustain his perspective.

I'm not sure what your future holds, but if you keep the phone lines open, I know it will "prosper and not harm you."

Stand at the Crossroads and Look:

1. Were you shocked to discover the context of the passage studied yesterday? Why?

2. What would you have expected the next verse to be about? Write out your own version of what you think Jeremiah 33:4–5 *should* say.

3. Does your version of the passage reflect God's perspective? Or yours?

4. Write out a prayer asking God to give you his perspective on your future.

5. What key lesson did you glean from today's study?

Truths to Stand Upon:

- From God's perspective, a great future is one in which we sustain his perspective.
- When we keep the phone line open to God, he will prosper and not harm us, no matter what circumstances we may face.

Day Three

Don't Assume Anything

I know, O Lord, that a man's life is not his own;
  it is not for man to direct his steps.

Jeremiah 10:23

I was so excited I thought I would burst. I was driving along in the car, minding my own business, when suddenly an idea came. *Give it to Janice*. Brilliant. I knew the idea was divinely inspired, direct from the throne room of God. I couldn't wait to put the plan into action.

Several years ago, I bought an expensive piece of equipment for my ministry. It was something I knew I just couldn't live without. Surprise! I used it exactly once, and then it sat around collecting dust in a closet. Now, at last, it would be put to good use. I was certain it was something Janice just couldn't live without. And when I gave it to her, she was going to be so blessed her joy would overflow. Such an expensive gift! I could just see the gratitude on her face already. In fact, she'd be so grateful, she'd probably want to be my new best friend.

The very next Sunday, I put the equipment in the car, but Janice wasn't at church. Bummer. Then the following week, Janice was at church but the equipment wasn't in the car. So I told her, in my most let's-build-some-excitement tone, that I had a wonderful surprise for her and I'd bring it the following week. She seemed pleased. I was thrilled.

Finally, the big moment came. Janice and the expensive equipment came face-to-face.

She was unmoved. She casually told me she didn't think she would have much use for it, but she was willing to take it off my hands. She paused and asked, "If I don't use it, do you want me to just give it back to you?" I fumbled for words then mumbled, "Um, yeah, sure."

I walked away crushed.

"But God, you TOLD ME to give it to her! This was YOUR idea and look how it turned out." I was baffled. Had I heard God wrong? Didn't he say what I thought he had said? It drove me nuts for several weeks, then it finally dawned on me. Yes, God had told me what to do, but he didn't tell me *why* he wanted me to do it. He told me what *action* to take, but he didn't tell me what *reaction* to expect. He never promised me the results I had hoped for.

God wanted my obedience, not my game plan. I just didn't have his perspective.

The longer I walk with God, the more convinced I am that I have absolutely *no idea* why he does half the things he does. I don't know why he creates newborn babies with deformities. I don't know why he lets five year olds die of leukemia. Or why he allows children to be molested and women to be raped. I don't know why good parents get rotten kids and rotten parents get good kids. I don't know why it always rains when you go on vacation. Or why people go to war in the name of God and why Christians invariably act like the biggest jerks in any given town.

I can't even figure out something simple like why he told me to give that expensive piece of equipment to Janice.

Let me tell you, if I were running the universe, things would be different. But you know what? I've recently come to an astonishing realization—and this has taken me quite a while—I'm not in charge of the universe.

God is.

I'm getting better at letting him do his job without interference or advice from me. I'm getting better at just doing what he tells me to do, without trying to guess the why. I'm getting better at practicing obedience and leaving the game plan to God. I'm learning not to jump to conclusions. I'm learning that "a woman's life is not her own; it is not for a woman to direct her steps." It's for a woman to follow wherever God directs, even if it doesn't make a bit of sense.

Stand at the Crossroads and Look:

1. Has God ever asked you to do something and you assumed you knew why, but your assumptions turned out to be all wrong? Describe.

2. What are some of the things about the way God runs the universe that don't make sense to you?

3. Is there something about the way God is currently directing your steps that doesn't make sense to you?

4. Write out a prayer acknowledging God's right to rule the universe and your life.

5. What key lesson did you glean from today's study?

Truths to Stand Upon:

- God wants our obedience, not our game plan.
- Follow wherever God directs, even if it doesn't make sense.

Day Four

God Does What He Pleases

"I say: My purpose WILL stand,
and I will do all that I please."

Isaiah 46:10 (emphasis added)

Earlier this week, I confessed that I almost always have an agenda. I think it's a woman thing. Take parties as a small example. Women never throw a Christmas party for the sake of throwing a Christmas party. That would be too simple. We have to invite Susie Single and Bob Bachelor because we just know they'll be perfect for each other and it's probably God's will for them to meet, get married, and ask us to be in the bridal party. We have an agenda.

Read through the following extended passage from John, chapter 11, noting the contrast between people's agendas and God's agenda:

> Now a man named Lazarus was sick. He was from Bethany, the village of Mary and her sister Martha. This Mary, whose brother Lazarus now lay sick, was the same one who poured perfume on the Lord and wiped his feet with her hair. So the sisters sent word to Jesus, "Lord, the one you love is sick."
>
> When he heard this, Jesus said, "This sickness will not end in death. No, it is for God's glory so that God's Son may be glorified through it." Jesus loved Martha and her sister and Lazarus. Yet when he heard that Lazarus was sick, he stayed where he was two more days.
>
> Then he said to his disciples, "Let us go back to Judea."
>
> "But Rabbi," they said, "a short while ago the Jews tried to stone you, and yet you are going back there?"
>
> Jesus answered, "Are there not twelve hours of daylight? A man who walks by day will not stumble, for he sees by this world's

light. It is when he walks by night that he stumbles, for he has no light."

After he had said this, he went on to tell them, "Our friend Lazarus has fallen asleep; but I am going there to wake him up."

His disciples replied, "Lord, if he sleeps, he will get better." Jesus had been speaking of his death, but his disciples thought he meant natural sleep.

So then he told them plainly, "Lazarus is dead, and for your sake I am glad I was not there, so that you may believe. But let us go to him."

Then Thomas (called Didymus) said to the rest of the disciples, "Let us also go, that we may die with him."

On his arrival, Jesus found that Lazarus had already been in the tomb for four days. Bethany was less than two miles from Jerusalem, and many Jews had come to Martha and Mary to comfort them in the loss of their brother. When Martha heard that Jesus was coming, she went out to meet him, but Mary stayed at home.

"Lord," Martha said to Jesus, "if you had been here, my brother would not have died. But I know that even now God will give you whatever you ask."

Jesus said to her, "Your brother will rise again."

Martha answered, "I know he will rise again in the resurrection at the last day."

Jesus said to her, "I am the resurrection and the life. He who believes in me will live, even though he dies; and whoever lives and believes in me will never die. Do you believe this?"

"Yes, Lord," she told him, "I believe that you are the Christ, the Son of God, who was to come into the world."

And after she had said this, she went back and called her sister Mary aside. "The Teacher is here," she said, "and is asking for you." When Mary heard this, she got up quickly and went to him. Now Jesus had not yet entered the village, but was still at the place where Martha had met him. When the Jews who had been with Mary in the house, comforting her, noticed how quickly she got up and went out, they followed her, supposing she was going to the tomb to mourn there.

When Mary reached the place where Jesus was and saw him, she fell at his feet and said, "Lord, if you had been here, my brother would not have died."

When Jesus saw her weeping, and the Jews who had come

along with her also weeping, he was deeply moved in spirit and troubled. "Where have you laid him?" he asked.

"Come and see, Lord," they replied.

Jesus wept.

Then the Jews said, "See how he loved him!"

But some of them said, "Could not he who opened the eyes of the blind man have kept this man from dying?"

Jesus, once more deeply moved, came to the tomb. It was a cave with a stone laid across the entrance. "Take away the stone," he said.

"But, Lord," said Martha, the sister of the dead man, "by this time there is a bad odor, for he has been there four days."

Then Jesus said, "Did I not tell you that if you believed, you would see the glory of God?"

So they took away the stone. Then Jesus looked up and said, "Father, I thank you that you have heard me. I knew that you always hear me, but I said this for the benefit of the people standing here, that they may believe that you sent me."

When he had said this, Jesus called in a loud voice, "Lazarus, come out!" The dead man came out, his hands and feet wrapped with strips of linen, and a cloth around his face.

Jesus said to them, "Take off the grave clothes and let him go."

Therefore many of the Jews who had come to visit Mary, and had seen what Jesus did, put their faith in him. But some of them went to the Pharisees and told them what Jesus had done. Then the chief priests and the Pharisees called a meeting of the Sanhedrin.

"What are we accomplishing?" they asked. "Here is this man performing many miraculous signs. If we let him go on like this, everyone will believe in him, and then the Romans will come and take away both our place and our nation."

Then one of them, named Caiaphas, who was high priest that year, spoke up, "You know nothing at all! You do not realize that it is better for you that one man die for the people than that the whole nation perish."

He did not say this on his own, but as high priest that year he prophesied that Jesus would die for the Jewish nation, and not only for that nation but also for the scattered children of God, to bring them together and make them one. So from that day on they plotted to take his life.

Stand at the Crossroads and Look:

1. What was the disciples' agenda? Was it the same as God's?

2. What was Thomas's perspective on God's agenda? Was he accurate?

3. What was Martha's agenda? Was it the same as God's?

4. What was Mary's agenda? Was it the same as God's?

5. What was the Pharisees' agenda? Was it the same as God's?

6. What was God's agenda?

7. Write out a prayer asking God to give you his perspective on this passage.

8. What key lesson did you glean from today's study?

Truths to Stand Upon:

- Even godly people can have agendas that conflict with God's agenda.
- Even ungodly people can have agendas that coincide with God's agenda.

Day Five

God's Purposes Will Stand

But the plans of the Lord stand firm forever,
the purposes of his heart through all generations.

Psalm 33:11

Today I want to give you my perspective on the John 11 passage. Hopefully, I can sustain God's perspective as I seek to do so.

Let's tackle the disciples first, because, bless their male hearts, their agenda is rather transparent. Their agenda is to keep Jesus alive. " 'But Rabbi,' they said, 'a short while ago the Jews tried to stone you, and yet you are going back there?' " (John 11:8). The motives behind their agenda are probably mixed. They love Jesus and don't want to see him harmed, but they also want him to be a Conquering Messiah. They want him to overthrow Roman rule and establish a Jewish kingdom. It goes without saying that they expect to play a vital part in this worldly kingdom.

Thomas appears more noble than the rest. Sort of sad that he's remembered for his moment of doubt (see John 20:24–29), rather than the bravery he demonstrates in this passage. At least he is willing to go and die with Jesus. But is that God's agenda? No. God wants Thomas and the other disciples to live and spread the Good News. Ultimately, ten of the twelve do, in fact, die a martyr's death. But not now. It's possible to have the right idea but the wrong timing. I think that's the case for Thomas.

Now Mary and Martha.

"So the sisters sent word to Jesus, 'Lord, the one you love is sick' " (John 11:3). The underlying premise is that if God really loves someone, he won't let him or her get sick, and if someone should happen to get sick, God will quickly provide healing. In other words, if God really loves us, he won't let us suffer. Period. This is a popular agenda in the church today, but I don't think it reflects God's perspective. I don't want to get into a theological debate here (we'll pursue the topic of suffering in greater detail during Week Eight). For now, just look at the book of Job. He was a righteous man who endured unspeakable suffering. Look at the prophets. Look at John the Baptist. Look at the early church and martyrs throughout history. For that matter, look at Jesus.

Back to the issue at hand. Mary and Martha wanted healing.[1] And they weren't too happy when they realized that Jesus hadn't gotten with the program:

> When Martha heard that Jesus was coming, she went out to meet him, but Mary stayed at home. "Lord," Martha said to Jesus, "if you had been here, my brother would not have died." (vv. 20–21)

I don't have proof, but I am convinced Martha said the previous statement *with an attitude*!

Mary and Martha wanted Lazarus' life to continue as it had always been. They tried desperately to keep their brother alive. Jesus wanted something completely different. He wanted death and resurrection. He wanted Lazarus' old life to vanish from the face of the earth so that he could have a whole *new life*. Restoring his old life would have required a miracle, to be sure. Giving him a new life required an even greater miracle. Every day, for the rest of Lazarus' life, he was a walking, talking testimony to the life-giving mercy of God. He was a living witness to the God of second chances.

Maybe you've been praying to God with an agenda for healing in your life. Maybe it's physical or emotional healing. Maybe it's the healing of a relationship. Is it possible that God is deliberately allowing that part of you to die? Allowing that part of your life to pass away? Maybe God is calling you out of your tomb. Out of that dead place where you've been dwelling for so long that the smell of death is upon you. Maybe, just maybe, God wants to give you something even greater than healing. Maybe he wants to give you a whole *new life*.

Now to the Pharisees. What was their agenda? They began

---

[1] I'm indebted to Martha Wilson for sharing this insight with me.

plotting to kill Jesus for the sake of a nation. And that's *exactly* what God had in mind. I think it's ironic that Jesus' closest friends were out of sync with God's agenda, while his enemies were on track. I'm not talking about their hearts, mind you. Martha's and Mary's hearts were in the right place; the Pharisees' hearts were completely corrupted by evil. Just goes to show that having your heart in the right place is *not* enough to ensure that you are pursuing God's agenda. We have to sustain his perspective as well.

The beautiful truth we need to hold on to as we leave this week is simply this: "But the plans of the Lord stand firm forever, the purposes of his heart through all generations" (Psalm 33:11). God knows what he's doing, and his plans are guaranteed to succeed. That's why it's so important for us to let go of our agenda and seek God's perspective.

Stand at the Crossroads and Look:

1. Is there something you are trying desperately to "keep alive"? Is it possible that God wants you to let it die, so that he can bring new life?

2. Does it surprise you that those who loved Jesus were out of sync with God's agenda, while his enemies were in sync? Does this truth have any significance for your life?

3. Do you find it a bit frightening to realize that having your heart in the right place is not enough to ensure you will always have God's agenda in view? Why or why not?

4. Write out a prayer asking God to enable you to keep your heart *and* your agenda in sync with his.

5. What key lesson did you glean from today's study?

6. Write out This Week's Verse from memory.

Truths to Stand Upon:

- It's possible that God wants to give you something greater than healing—a whole new life.
- Having our heart in the right place is not enough to ensure we are pursuing God's agenda. We must sustain his perspective as well.

Weekly Review:

Take a few moments to fill in the ten actions and attitudes required to Stand Firm. Look in the back of the book if you need help.

S _____ God first

S _____ God's perspective

S _____ your spiritual hunger

S _____ the love God has for you

S _____ yourself against the attacks of the enemy

S _____ truth to yourself and others

S _____ the tide of mediocrity

S _____ like a saint

S _____ wholeheartedly

S _____ firm until the end

WEEK THREE:
Satisfy Your Spiritual Hunger

This Week's Verse:

Your words are what sustain me; they are food to my hungry
soul. They bring joy to my sorrowing heart and delight me.
How proud I am to bear your name, O Lord.

Jeremiah 15:16 (TLB)

Day One

How Hungry Are You?

Your words are what sustain me; they are food to my hungry soul. They bring joy to my sorrowing heart and delight me. How proud I am to bear your name, O Lord.

Jeremiah 15:16 (TLB)

At the risk of giving away the plain truth about what a "hick" I've become, I can't resist another story about the saga of our dogs in the mountains. I've mentioned that because they foolishly abused their freedom, we had to cage them. Naturally, they commenced barking. Our neighbors weren't happy about that either. We needed a new strategy.

So we bought an electronic fence.

We created an artificial perimeter around our property, and then we placed "hot-wired" collars on the dogs. Now if the poor wretches attempted to leave the premises, they literally got the shock of their lives. The other place we electronically declared off limits was the chicken coop. Stinker is half-retriever, and we had already learned a painful lesson about where the term "bird-dog" originated. So the dogs stopped barking, the chickens were safe, the neighbors were happy, and the dumb dogs we got for "free" had now cost us a small fortune. But all was well in the universe.

Or so we thought.

Unbeknownst to us—and the dogs—the power supply on the electronic fence had malfunctioned. We never noticed because the dogs continued to stay within the perimeter. The dogs never noticed because they had learned, by painful experience, not to test the perimeter.

Then one day it happened. Stinker got hungry for chicken. Real hungry. And in what I can only guess was a gutsy moment of sheer abandon, he went charging toward the chicken coop and discovered that the boundary line holding him back no longer existed.

I have no way of knowing how many months had passed since the power supply was cut off. Perhaps Stinker could have sauntered across the border long before he did. It wasn't until he got hungry, really hungry, that he decided to test his limits. He didn't even attempt to break free until there was something he desperately wanted on the other side.

Are you living inside boundaries that no longer have the power to hold you back? Maybe you've stayed within your comfort zone so long that it's never even occurred to you that there's something more out there.

It's time to let yourself *feel* the hunger. And no matter what it is that you *think* you're hungry for, your real hunger is for God himself. God alone can satisfy your inner cravings. Nothing can fill your heart like God's Word, but you've got to want it more than anything else on this earth. You've got to come to the place Stinker came to, where plain old dog food just won't do.

If you're fed up with dog food, with cheap substitutes for truth, if you've had enough "fillers" and "artificial flavors," if you've had enough of the junk we fill our schedules with hoping to find satisfaction, then you're ready for Real Food. It's time to make a mad dash through your self-created boundary lines and feast on what your soul is hungering for—the Word of God.

C.S. Lewis observed that "the less the Bible is read, the more it is translated." If that doesn't sum up the church in America today, I don't know what does. Adding more translations and versions (you know, like The Barbeque Lover's Bible) is a cheap substitute for the real thing—reading one of the countless Bibles you already have.

So . . . how hungry are you? Hungry enough to challenge your limits? Like the limit that says you couldn't possibly wake up thirty minutes earlier to read his Word? Like the limit that says you can't possibly set aside one day a week to attend a Bible study? Like the limit that says you'll never finish this ten-week journey?

I'm here to tell you that God has cut off the power supply behind those limitations. In fact, he did it a long time ago—the day Jesus died on the cross to set you free.

There's another power at work in your life now—the power to move beyond the world you've known. The question is: Are you hungry enough to go for it?

Stand at the Crossroads and Look:

1. What are some of the self-imposed limitations that have been holding you back from feasting on God's Word?

2. How might you break through those limits?

3. What is it that you *think* you're hungry for? Clue: Whatever would finish the phrase, "If only . . ." is what you think you're hungry for.

4. Can you think of a time when you truly hungered for more of God? For more of his Word? Describe.

5. Write out a prayer asking God to show you that his Word—and a relationship with him—is the only thing that will truly satisfy your hunger.

6. What key lesson did you glean from today's study?

Truths to Stand Upon:

- We live within self-imposed boundaries because we haven't bothered to test the limits.
- Crash through your self-imposed boundaries and feast on what your soul is really hungering for—the Word of God.

Day Two

What Are You Eating?

Let us purify ourselves from everything that contaminates body and spirit, perfecting holiness out of reverence for God.

2 Corinthians 7:1

For the past year or so, a new college campus has been under construction within walking distance of my home. It's been fascinating to watch the progress, so I often wandered around, peeking into windows to see what's new. One day, while exploring the campus on one of my fact-finding missions, I noticed that they had filled a room with weight-lifting equipment.

I'm not sure what came over me, but I decided right then and there to sign up for the weight-lifting class. And since I've always prided myself on being an A student, I threw myself into the class with abandon. Midway through the semester, my teacher made a comment to me that really got my attention.

"Donna," he said. "You are one of the most dedicated students in this class. You're in here every day. You're putting in a lot of hours; you're pushing your limits in terms of how much weight you can lift. I mean, I've gotta tell you, you're really doing a great job."

I smiled.

He paused. Then he raised his eyebrows in a puzzled fashion, looked me over from head to toe, and continued, "But you know, it's kinda strange. *You don't really look much better!*"

I stopped smiling.

He paused again. "With the amount of effort you've been putting in, you should have seen more improvement by now. Tell me, what have you been eating?"

Uh-oh. Suddenly I was whisked back in time to my days as a

Catholic schoolgirl sitting in the confessional with the priest waiting patiently for me to spill my guts.

I began with the good part. Well, I thought it was the good part. "The day starts out great. I play this little game where I see how long I can go without a drop of food. I can usually make it until almost noon."

He didn't look happy. I thought maybe he wanted me to cut to the serious sins. "I honestly don't eat that much," I insisted, trying to think of a way to hide my bulging thighs from his skinny little gaze. "I don't eat practically anything all day. Okay, maybe I pig out before I go to bed, but I figure I've got lots of unused calories to use up."

"That's your problem right there!" he declared triumphantly. "You're not eating enough."

"Not eating enough? I've been killing myself to *avoid* eating, and you're telling me to eat *more?*"

He proceeded to explain truths I had learned years earlier but had somehow lost sight of. If you want to be healthy, you've got to feed your body the right foods. And you have to feed it often. I switched to a new program where I eat small meals every three hours all day long. And you know what? I've never felt better in my life. As a bonus, I can handle the weight lifting with much greater ease and grace.

All the weight lifting in the world is no substitute for the right food.

I think I've made the same mistake in my spiritual life. Maybe you have, too. I want to do the "heavy lifting." The exciting, challenging stuff like evangelism, teaching, organizing women's retreats, trying to change *other people's* lives.

While I worked myself to exhaustion, getting little results, God quietly looked on, posing the question, "Donna, what are you eating?" Sadly, the answer is the same one I gave my weight-lifting instructor—not nearly enough.

Have you been playing a little game with the Christian life, seeing how long you can go without spiritual food? You'll never make serious progress like that. You need to eat first thing in the morning and continue feeding your spirit throughout the day. How does every three hours sound?

Since I've found that planning out my meals in advance makes it easier for me to stick with the program (both physically and spiritually), let me encourage you to think about what you're going to eat and to plan accordingly. Your small spiritual meals might include reading God's Word, a lesson in this book, worshiping along with praise music, praying with a friend over the phone, writing out a prayer to God, tuning in to the daily broadcast of your favorite Bible teacher on Christian radio. Ask God to show you the food that's right for you . . . then dig in and start eating. You'll find the heavy lifting isn't so heavy when you've given your spirit the fuel it requires.[1]

Stand at the Crossroads and Look:

1. Do you prefer heavy lifting to fueling your body? Why?

2. What have been the results of your spiritual malnutrition?

---

[1]While I recognize that not everyone has the time or inclination to pursue physical fitness, I also recognize that it is a major concern for many women. I don't want to make anyone feel guilty here. You may be working all day outside the home and/or have three small children to chase. The program I use may feel overwhelming to you. If it does, don't worry about it. What matters is loving God and loving people. The rest is just details. With that caveat in mind, here goes: Over the past several months, as I've shared today's lesson at women's conferences, it has become a real favorite. Women sit up in their chairs when I mention that I was pushing size 12 and am now down to a size 6. Hey, don't hate me because I've lost weight! First of all, because I've worked incredibly hard to make it happen. But most importantly, because I have decided to let you in on the little secret I've shared with the ladies at my conferences. Now these ladies are e-mailing me about all the weight they are losing and how great they feel. Okay, the secret is *Body for Life* (1-800-297-9776 or www.bodyforlife.com), a program that includes weight lifting, cardiovascular training, and a strict dietary regimen. I highly recommend that you read the book, visit the website, and commit to a 120-day experiment to see if it works for you. It worked for me and I've never felt more invigorated. I won't go into any details here because my editor is concerned with "tangents." Suffice it to say that Body for Life is a fabulous program!

3. Plan out some "spiritual meals."

4. Write out a prayer confessing your neglect of spiritual food and asking God to send you spiritual "hunger pangs" when it's time to eat.

5. What key lesson did you glean from today's study?

Truths to Stand Upon:

- "Heavy lifting" is ineffective if we fail to eat the right spiritual food with the right frequency.
- Aim for small spiritual meals throughout the day.

Day Three

What Are You Hungry For?

Do not be deceived: God cannot be mocked. A man reaps what he sows. The one who sows to please his sinful nature, from that nature will reap destruction; the one who sows to please the Spirit, from the Spirit will reap eternal life. Let us not become weary in doing good, for at the proper time we will reap a harvest if we do not give up.

Galatians 6:7–9

When I was outlining this book and chose today's passage, I had planned to tell you the tale of three gardens. We conducted a home-school experiment last year using three different types of soil for three different gardens. One we dug deep, one was shallow, one midway between the two. For two of the gardens we used regular water; one was drenched daily in water saturated with duck manure. I was going to tell you how that all worked out, and the lessons we learned, and how we noticed that our garden didn't grow anything we didn't first plant.

Reaping. Sowing. That sort of thing.

But I've changed my mind. I'm not going to tell you about the three gardens. I think you have enough sense to figure it out for yourself. And you've no doubt heard hundreds of gardening illustrations. Jesus used gardening illustrations because he lived in an agricultural society. We don't. So let's ditch the gardening talk and chat about something really important: junk food.

I'm sitting here in my office, alone on a Saturday night, writing a book filled with profound spiritual insights. Well, at least I hope it's filled with profound spiritual insights. I have gentle praise music playing in the background, an aromatic candle burning brightly on the table beside me, and a cup of hot apple cider on my desk. Talk about your inspirational environments! Ah, writer's heaven. (I decided not to mention that my neighbor's toddler has been screaming at the top of her lungs for two solid hours. I wouldn't want to spoil your sense of the ambience.)

Anyway, can you guess what I'm thinking about in the midst of all this inspiration?

Donuts.

Chocolate-covered donuts, to be exact.

Truth be told, I've been thinking about chocolate-covered donuts since I woke up this morning. That's twelve solid hours of donut fixation. I think I may be suffering from obsessive-compulsive disorder. They sell them (the donuts, not obsessive-compulsive disorders) at the local grocery store, and it's still open for a few more hours. I'm thinking I could brush my hair, throw on some clothes, and dash on over there real quick, and no one would be the wiser. It would be my little secret. Yes. A donut would be just the thing right now.

Yet, I am standing firm. I am not going to buy that donut. And I'll tell you why. It's because I spent an hour and a half working out in the gym this afternoon. Did you know it takes forty-five minutes on the treadmill to burn off two Oreo cookies? A donut probably takes twice the time. Now that I'm making an effort in a positive direction, I can honestly say that junk food is less tempting.

There's another factor at play here, too. Not only is my mind working for me, but my body is, too. Something has changed within me. I used to be able to polish off an entire bag of Oreos in one sitting. No kidding. Now, if I eat more than a handful, I feel sick to my stomach. My body doesn't want it, even if my taste buds do. I've noticed that *my body literally rejects junk* because it has become accustomed to my new, healthier eating patterns.

I think this principle holds true in the spiritual realm as well. As we develop our spiritual taste buds by feeding ourselves a healthier diet, we have less desire for junk food. And when those old cravings come calling, we have more power to resist. You'll also notice changes in your appetite. Things you once consumed greedily, like romance novels, will lose their appeal. Your spirit will cry out, "Yuck! Gross me out already! Feed me something *real.*"

Just like I'm resisting that donut that's been calling my name all day, you'll find it easier to resist soap operas, stupid jokes, and idle phone conversations. Your spirit just won't tolerate that kind of junk food anymore.

But don't start by resisting. That won't work. Start by feeding yourself the *right stuff*. Read your Bible every day without fail. Then carve out time for other uplifting Christian books. Check out *The Christian's Secret of a Happy Life* by Hannah Whitall Smith. Next, try *Stepping Heavenward* by Elizabeth Prentiss and anything you can get your hands on by Andrew Murray.[2] Surround yourself with "the great cloud of witnesses," by reading missionary biographies like *Peace Child* by Don Richardson or *A Chance to Die: The Life and Legacy of Amy Carmichael* by Elisabeth Elliot. If you can track down Helen Roseveare's autobiography, *Give Me This Mountain* (InterVarsity Press), it will change your life forever. It did mine.

I think anything written by Corrie Ten Boom or Ruth Bell Graham is just extraordinary. What incredible women of God, and brilliant communicators to boot. If you can handle something absolutely radical, try *Traveling Mercies* by Anne Lamott. I roared with laughter through the whole thing. Well, when I wasn't crying I was laughing. She's totally unconventional (brace yourself for profanities and wild antics, and don't say I didn't warn you), but she is as real as real gets and she can write like nobody's business. I wish I had a fraction of her talent.

Feed your *other senses*, as well. We are such slaves to our taste buds, it's ridiculous. Feast your eyes. Make your home a beautiful place. If you can't make your whole house beautiful, pick a room. My house is a perpetual wreck, but my prayer room is always neat and it's flat-out gorgeous. Brightly painted. Lovely Victorian pictures on the wall. Flowered couch. Pretty pillows. A little table covered in white lace with a flower arrangement and candle on top. Next to my "God chair"[3] is my prayer basket containing my Bible, prayer journal, and all the books I'm currently working on.

I spend time in my prayer room because it feeds my spirit.

---

[2]Bethany House publishes many of Andrew Murray's books. Call 1-800-328-6109 for more information.

[3]That's what my daughter Tara calls my rocking chair because it's the place I like to sit when I talk to God. Do you have a special chair like that? You should. When my children awake in the morning, the first place they look for me is in my prayer room. Whatever else I'm doing wrong as a parent, I think I'm sending the right message about this. Where do your children look for you? In front of the TV set? By the telephone? Think about it.

What about your sense of touch? Hug someone! Treat yourself to a massage, rather than a box of Godiva. Take cozy baths and let Calgon take you away while you read your missionary biography! How about your sense of smell? Feast on scented candles. I like Yankee brand the best, because they seem the most aromatic. To please your sense of hearing, play uplifting praise music. Right now, I'm listening to *Inspirational Piano Moods* (Straightway Music, 1999), which was sent to me as a gift from one of my Canadian readers named Margaret. What a blessing it has been!

My sisters, you need to be feeding your spirit good, quality food like this. I guarantee your taste buds will begin to take a back seat as you nourish your spirit through ALL the senses God has granted you. Your spirit will adjust and your cravings for spiritual junk will gradually subside. Not disappear, mind you. Subside.

The key is to stick with it. "The one who sows to please the Spirit, from the Spirit will reap eternal life. Let us not become weary in doing good, for at the proper time we will reap a harvest if we do not give up."

Stand at the Crossroads and Look:

1. What have you been feeding your spirit?

2. What *should* you be feeding your spirit?

3. List some ideas you would like to incorporate, either from the chapter or your own reflection, on how you might feed your spirit through a variety of your senses.

4. Write out a prayer committing yourself to the careful cultivation of your spirit.

5. What key lesson did you glean from today's study?

Truths to Stand Upon:

- As you feed your spirit a healthy diet, your cravings for mental junk food will subside.
- Feed your spirit through the variety of your senses: sight, sound, touch, and smell.

Day Four

Feasting on the Whole Counsel of God

For everything that was written in the past was written to teach us, so that through endurance and the encouragement of the Scriptures we might have hope.

Romans 15:4

Okay, so we've figured out that woman cannot live on spiritual donuts alone. Unfortunately, even those of us who have moved beyond junk food often eat the same stuff day after day. In some parts of the world, people don't have much choice: They are lucky to get bread and water or rice and beans on a routine basis. I once met a beautiful young MK (missionary kid) who was raised in the Peruvian jungle until her late teen years. When she came to America for the first time during her parents' furlough, they sent her into a grocery store to buy cereal. Big mistake, Mom and Dad. The poor girl just about had a nervous breakdown right there in Aisle 9. In Peru, cereal is cereal. One box. No choice. In America, cereal is a billion-dollar industry.

Nevertheless, even with the vast array of food choices available to us, most Americans tend to get stuck in dietary ruts. Chances are, of the zillions of brands and flavors available, you eat the same cereal every day. And I'll bet you've been eating the same one for years. I'll fess up—for me, it's Kellogg's Special K. Day in. Day out. Lunch is a no-brainer, too. For the under-twelve crowd, it's peanut butter and jelly. A grilled cheese sandwich or pizza if they are lucky enough to get a hot meal. Teenagers eat Burger King or Taco Bell. Every day. Come dinnertime, most of us go for meat and potatoes or a casserole. It becomes a routine, and we find ourselves eating the same handful of meals, week after week.

Jesus noted, "Man does not live on bread alone, but on EVERY word that comes from the mouth of God" (Matthew 4:4, emphasis added). Today's verse points out: "EVERYTHING that was written in the past was written to teach us." Second Timothy 3:16–17 reminds us that "ALL Scripture is God-breathed and is useful for teaching, rebuking, correcting and training in righteousness, so that the man of God may be thoroughly equipped for every good work" (emphasis added).

Every. Everything. All. Getting the picture? Not just a few favorite verses and pet passages. Not the same old, same old. Every word. Everything that was written. All Scripture.

There are places in the world where the whole church shares one Bible. Entire "people groups" have only a portion of the Scriptures in their native tongue. These believers have no choice: bread and butter, rice and beans. We've got all of Aisle 9, not to mention the rest of the grocery store and Super Wal-Mart.

God has set before us a smorgasbord of spiritual food. So why do we eat the same stuff over and over again? "I don't understand the book of Revelation. Whatever's gonna happen is gonna happen." "The Old Testament is irrelevant. We're not under all those weird laws anyway. Besides, who cares who begat who?" "Paul's letters are soooo long-winded. I don't want to get bogged down in all that dry doctrine anyway. I like to read the Psalms."

There's a real danger in being such finicky eaters, my friends. We'll miss out on all the rich morsels hidden throughout. There's something special in *every* book in the Bible. For example, did you know that Christ is portrayed in each and every book? Consider this:

In Genesis, he is the seed of the woman
In Exodus, he is the Passover Lamb
In Leviticus, he is the atoning sacrifice
In Numbers, he is the bronze serpent lifted up in the desert
In Deuteronomy, he is the prophet Moses saw
In Joshua, he is the captain of the army
In Judges, he is my deliverer
In Ruth and Esther, he is our Kinsman-Redeemer
In 1 and 2 Samuel, 1 and 2 Kings, and 1 and 2 Chronicles, he is the Promised King
In Ezra and Nehemiah, he is the restorer of the nations

In Job, he is my Redeemer
In Psalms, he is my all in all
In Proverbs, he is my pattern
In Ecclesiastes, he is my goal
In Song of Songs, he is the lily of the valley, the bright and morning star
In the major and minor prophets, he is the Promised King yet to come
In Matthew, he is the reigning King
In Mark, he is the servant
In Luke, he is a man
In John, he is very God
In Acts, he is ascending, seated, and sending the Holy Spirit
In the letters, he is Christ filling and indwelling the church
In Revelation, he is Christ returning and reigning.[4]

I'll bet you didn't know that, did you? It just goes to show that "*all Scripture* is God-breathed" and "*everything that was written* in the past was written to teach us." Okay, so here's the challenge. Read through your entire Bible. *This year*. It's the same challenge I set forth in every book I write, but have you taken me up on the challenge yet?

If you would truly satisfy your spiritual hunger, then you must feast on the *whole counsel* of God.

Stand at the Crossroads and Look:

1. Have you read through the entire Bible? I mean, straight through, front to finish, in order?

---

[4]Transcribed from the audiocassette, "A Symphony for the Soul" by Charles Swindoll. Insight for Living, 1978. If you'd like to order Pastor Swindoll's series of teachings through the entire Bible, entitled "God's Masterwork," call 1-800-772-8888 or check out their website: www.insight.org. The cost is around $230, and worth every penny. I acquired the whole collection one "occasion" at a time: one for my birthday, another for Christmas, etc. It took a year or so, but I wasn't reading through the Bible any faster than that anyway.

2. Do you tend to eat the same spiritual food over and over again? What portion do you munch on most often? Why?

3. Do you see the importance of expanding your menu selections?

4. Write out a prayer of commitment to read through the entire Bible in the next twelve months.

5. What key lesson did you glean from today's study?

Truths to Stand Upon:

- There's something to feast upon in *every* book of the Bible.
- If you would truly satisfy your spiritual hunger, then you must feast on the *whole counsel* of God.

Day Five

Keep Your Spiritual Fervor

Never be lacking in zeal, but keep your spiritual fervor, serving the Lord.

Romans 12:11

Just to whet your spiritual appetite for feasting on the whole counsel of God, I thought I'd share a tremendously encouraging Old Testament story that may have escaped your notice. The following account is taken from Joshua, chapter 14:

Now the men of Judah approached Joshua at Gilgal, and Caleb son of Jephunneh the Kenizzite said to him, "You know what the Lord said to Moses the man of God at Kadesh Barnea about you and me. I was forty years old when Moses the servant of the Lord sent me from Kadesh Barnea to explore the land. And I brought him back a report according to my convictions, but my brothers who went up with me made the hearts of the people melt with fear. I, however, followed the Lord my God wholeheartedly. So on that day Moses swore to me, 'The land on which your feet have walked will be your inheritance and that of your children forever, because you have followed the Lord my God wholeheartedly.'

"Now then, just as the Lord promised, he has kept me alive for forty-five years since the time he said this to Moses, while Israel moved about in the desert. *So here I am today, eighty-five years old! (Emphasis added. Think about an eighty-five-year-old man you know; then try to imagine him asking permission to go out into battle.)* I am still as strong today as the day Moses sent me out; I'm just as vigorous to go out to battle now as I was then. Now give me this hill country that the Lord promised me that day. You yourself heard then that the Anakites were there and their cities were large and fortified, but, the Lord helping me, I will drive them out just as he said."

Then Joshua blessed Caleb son of Jephunneh and gave him Hebron as his inheritance. So Hebron has belonged to Caleb son of Jephunneh the Kenizzite ever since, because he followed the Lord, the God of Israel, wholeheartedly." (Joshua 14:6–14)

Most of the eighty-five year olds I know can't even *climb* a hill, yet Caleb wanted to go up and *fight* in the hills. Far from rocking in his easy chair, he wanted to go where the battle was the toughest. He wanted to fight where the enemy was strongest.

Commenting on the life of Caleb, J. Oswald Sanders wrote: "Perhaps we, too, should remove our slippers and attack some menacing mountain in which the enemies of God are entrenched."

Then he recounts some examples of people who demonstrate spiritual fervor later in life:

C.H. Nash, who founded the Melbourne Bible Institute and trained 1,000 young men and women for Christian service, retired his principalship at the age of 70. At 80, he received assurance from the Lord that a further fruitful ministry of 10 years lay ahead of him. This assurance was abundantly fulfilled. During those years he was uniquely blessed in a ministry of Bible teaching to key groups of clergy and laymen, probably the most fruitful years of his life. When he was nearly 90, this author found him completing the reading of Volume 6 of Toynbee's monumental history as a mental exercise.

Mr. Benjamin Ryrie retired as a missionary of the China Inland Mission when he reached the age of 70. When he was 80, he decided to learn New Testament Greek, as he had not had the opportunity when he was younger. He became proficient in reading and teaching the Greek New Testament. At 90, he attended a refresher course in New Testament at the Toronto Theological Seminary.[5]

This past week, one of the members of our weekly women's Bible study went home to be with the Lord. Her name was Emily Beers. She was seventy-four years old. During the spring term, our leader taught my previous study, *Walking in Total God-Confidence*, and had

---

[5]Adapted from "Joshua: Triumph after Tragedy." A sermon by Charles Swindoll. Insight for Living, copyright 1979.

each member complete the Participant Profile Sheet. On Thursday, she read Emily's profile to the class. These were Emily's goals: "I hope to learn to memorize more and to be inspired to refer more to the Bible. To be more relaxed and comfortable with speaking about my Lord."

I just sat and wept as I realized that my book was part of the final months of Emily's life journey. This evening, I found a letter Emily wrote to me when she had finished the study... and I wept again. Her words filled me with joy, but they also gave me a great sense of urgency, realizing that *this book* may be the last tool God uses in someone's life. That's just mind-boggling and tremendously humbling to me.

I also cried tears of admiration. When I'm seventy-four, I hope I'm still attending a weekly women's Bible study, seeking to satisfy my spiritual hunger, and desiring to serve God fervently. I'll never forget delivering a talk at a small Women's Aglow meeting in New Jersey. A ninety-two-year-old woman sat in the front row *taking notes*. It blew me out of the water. I knew there was nothing I could say to her that was worth writing down. But she took notes anyway. She wasn't listening to me. She was listening wholeheartedly to God, eager to learn and grow wherever she could.

If you're in the second half of your life, wondering what a continued life of spiritual fervor and satisfying your spiritual hunger might look like, my dear friend Brenda Poinsett has written a helpful book, *What Will I Do With the Rest of My Life?* (www.navpress.com or 1-800-366-7788).

Keep your spiritual fervor.

Stand at the Crossroads and Look:

1. How did you feel when you realized that Caleb was *eighty-five years old* when he asked permission to go out and fight the enemies of God? Note your reaction to today's passage.

2. If you are in the second half of life, how are you currently demonstrating spiritual fervor?

3. What changes, if any, do you need to make?

4. If you are in the first half of life, what foundation can you lay now to ensure that you maintain your spiritual fervor? What would you like to do in the second half of your life?

5. Can you think of someone in the second half of life whose spiritual fervor in serving the Lord is worth knowing about? Write his or her story and be prepared to tell it to someone this week. (Your class, if you are involved in one. If not, just share it with a friend.)

6. Write out a prayer expressing your desire to "keep your spiritual fervor, serving the Lord."

7. What key lesson did you glean from today's study?

8. Write out This Week's Verse from memory.

Truths to Stand Upon:

- The life of Caleb is a beautiful example of someone who maintained spiritual fervor serving the Lord.
- Whatever God has called you to do, no matter your age, serve him wholeheartedly.

Weekly Review:

Take a few moments to fill in the ten actions and attitudes required to Stand Firm. Look in the back of the book if you need help.

S _____ God first

S _____ God's perspective

S _____ your spiritual hunger

S _____ the love God has for you

S _____ yourself against the attacks of the enemy

S _____ truth to yourself and others

S _____ the tide of mediocrity

S _____ like a saint

S _____ wholeheartedly

S _____ firm until the end

WEEK FOUR:
Savor the Love God Has for You

This Week's Verse:

"So now I have sworn not to be angry with you . . .
Though the mountains be shaken
and the hills be removed,
yet my unfailing love for you will not be shaken
nor my covenant of peace be removed,"
says the Lord, who has compassion on you.

Isaiah 54:9–10

Day One

Unfailing Love

"So now I have sworn not to be angry with you . . .
Though the mountains be shaken,
*   and the hills be removed,*
yet my unfailing love for you will not be shaken
*   nor my covenant of peace be removed,"*
says the Lord, who has compassion on you.

Isaiah 54:9–10

God uses the weirdest things to teach us sometimes. I thought seriously about entitling today's lesson "One Dead Car and a Flock of Dead Chickens" but then y'all would know I was seriously crazy. But, truth be told, that's what it's about: one dead car and a flock of dead chickens.

Here's how the tale begins. I had put together the prayer list to end all prayer lists. I mean, this was the list of stuff God had better take care of or else my world was gonna come to an end. High on the list was "Please go before me to the car dealer. Grant me favor in their eyes so that I get a great deal on a great car." Now, God knew I needed a new car. It was past time to replace my rickety old Volvo, which I affectionately referred to as my "Trash Can on Wheels." I live in the desert, and the car had no air conditioning. Now, I could conceivably survive. In fact, I managed to survive well into the summer. But do you know what it does to a mother's heart to hear crying in the back seat as two little girls suffer through 113-degree heat?

It wasn't that I wanted a car; I NEEDED a car.

Are you with me? If so, nod your head and repeat after me: "Girl, you NEEDED a car." Your words will fly off into the spirit realm and travel across the miles to comfort me.

Another item high on the list was "Empower me to be a joyful, effective mother." Now for me, a big part of being a joyful, effective mother is keeping everyone—from kids to critters—alive. I mean, that's got to be ground level, right?

Okay, the stage is set. We've established that God knew what I needed. Now it gets ugly.

Exactly one week after I bought the new car—the one I had spent months praying for—it died in the middle of the road. I guess I should have been thankful that we were all alive, but I was too focused on how furious I was at God.

All I asked for was a decent car—*is this DIFFICULT?* What kind of a God can't help a mom get a good deal on a good car? Oh, I was hot. And not because of the weather. I was furious, I mean furious, with God.

Then I was furious with the car dealer. I called, complained, and they said, "No problem. Bring it back in, and we'll set you up with a new car you'll feel more confident about."

I called a cease-fire with God and the car dealer.

It was short-lived.

I drove the two hours to the dealer and sat down optimistically. "Okay, Mrs. Partow," the salesman began to slither, "I've run the numbers for you. The car you bought was actually worth $4,000 less than you paid for it, so we'll be willing to buy it back at the lower price and use that as a down-payment toward a new car."

EXCUSE ME!!!!!!!!!!!

Obviously, I couldn't afford to trade the car in at an instant $4,000 loss. So I had no choice but to drive home, stewing in the knowledge that I had grossly overpaid for a car I couldn't rely upon. You know, the car I had spent MONTHS praying God would get me a good deal on.

Hostilities resumed with a vengeance. I wasn't even speaking to God.

Then it happened. A few days later, I pulled into my property and was met with a heartbreaking sight: The place was literally strewn with dead chickens. Feathers and body parts were everywhere. The dogs' electronic fence malfunctioned again, and Stinker had wiped out almost our entire flock of chickens and my precious rooster. I sat in the midst of the mayhem, weeping uncontrollably, crying out over and over, "I just wanted to be a good mother. I just wanted to be a good mother."

I had tried so hard to make our home a warm, wonderful place, and for me, the chickens were an integral part of the lifestyle I wanted to create. What could be better for kids than going out to gather fresh eggs for breakfast each morning? In my opinion, fresh eggs were quintessential "good mothering." Maybe that sounds pathetic, but the loss of our chickens symbolized a much greater loss.

And maybe this sounds stupid, too, but I'll say it anyway: I truly loved my rooster. Each morning, I would awaken to the beautiful sound of his crowing. It was my daily call to prayer. I'd get up and head downstairs to my "God chair," where I'd sit reading my Bible and praying (for important stuff like a car that runs and animals that stay alive) until the children awoke. Then I'd hold them in my arms and pray for each of them as we began a new day.

Now I overslept and my God chair sat vacant.

I began to wonder if God even existed and why I ever bothered to dedicate so much of my life—my time, my energy, my love—to him.

Then I defied him. I went off and deliberately disobeyed him.

As the reality of what I had done began to dawn on me, I became angry with myself. I wanted to turn back to God, but now that I had failed him, I was certain the tables had turned, that now *he* was angry with *me*.

I spent an entire Saturday crying out to God, asking him if he was disappointed in me. Angry with me.

As I sat in church the next day, June 18, 2000, my eyes drifted down to where my Bible lay open. Isaiah 54:9–10 leapt off the page:

"So now I have sworn not to be angry with you . . .
Though the mountains be shaken
   and the hills be removed,
yet my unfailing love for you will not be shaken
   nor my covenant of peace be removed,"
says the Lord, who has compassion on you.

Right there in the second to the last pew, God revealed himself in a new and personal way. I have never loved him more than I did at that moment. He had never been more real.

As I reflected on the journey that had just unfolded, I realized that it revealed a pattern that has repeated itself over and over in my life. Perhaps in yours, as well?

Phase 1. I become angry with God
Phase 2. I begin to doubt his existence
Phase 3. I turn my back on him
Phase 4. I stumble, then become angry with myself
Phase 5. I am afraid God is angry with me, that I've committed the unpardonable sin
Phase 6. God calls me back, revealing himself in a new and personal way

The next time I decide to get angry with God, I'm hoping to skip Phases 2 through 5, and watch for Phase 6. I just wish I could learn the easy way. Instead, it took one dead car and a flock of dead chickens for me to see these truths. Like I said, God uses the weirdest things to teach us sometimes.

Stand at the Crossroads and Look:

1. Have you ever become angry with God? Describe the circumstances.

2. What was the outcome of your anger?

3. Did it cause you to doubt his existence?

4. Did it lead you to turn your back on him? Describe.

5. Did turning your back on God cause you to stumble? How so?

6. Since you are reading this book, I assume you eventually turned back to God! What prompted you to do so?

7. Write out a prayer thanking God for his unfailing love.

8. What key lesson did you glean from today's study?

Truths to Stand Upon:

- God has sworn not to be angry with us.
- Though the mountains be shaken and the hills be removed, God's unfailing love for us can never be shaken.

Day Two

When God Came Down

The Lord is my light and my salvation—
  whom shall I fear?
The Lord is the stronghold of my life—
  of whom shall I be afraid?
Though an army besiege me,
  my heart will not fear;
though war break out against me,
  even then will I be confident.
I am still confident of this:
  I will see the goodness of the Lord
  in the land of the living.
Wait for the Lord;
  be strong and take heart
  and wait for the Lord.

Psalm 27:1, 3, 13–14

Sometimes God's goodness seems far away, doesn't it? Even though we read of his love, even though we catch glimpses of it, when circumstances are dark, it's hard to see his light. And because we can't see him, it's hard to rest in his love when we're facing a crisis. Somehow we want—even need—to experience human love. We savor human comfort and reassurance more than we savor the love of God. While there's nothing wrong with seeking human comfort, we're on dangerous ground when we run to people instead of God. That's another lesson I learned the hard way.

It began with a call from my daughter Nikki, who was 3,000 miles away at college.[1] She had just talked, by phone, with a counselor from

---

[1] If you read *Walking in Total God-Confidence*, you may recall Nikki's story. Nikki came to live with us when she was twelve years old, when her mom and dad went to prison. Although we are not biologically or legally bound, I have always referred to her as my daughter.

our church, whom I had turned to in a last-ditch plea for help in coping with a family crisis, As I had sat in his office a few days earlier, I thought to myself, "Here at last is someone I can count on." I had been running here, there, and everywhere looking desperately for solutions. I ran to this church official and that church counselor. I ran to experts, family, and friends. I wanted someone to hear me, help me, rescue me from the nightmare my life had become.

Now Nikki had to share news she knew would break my heart. She spoke gently. "He didn't believe you. He just didn't believe you. I'm so sorry."

I was stunned. Blown away. Physically reeling in shock. I set down the phone, walked out on my front deck, and screamed at the top of my lungs. "GOOOOOOOOOOOOD, where are you?" I must have screamed for five minutes. When I finally returned to the phone, my daughter tried comforting me. "I told him the truth about what's really been going on. I think he believed me," she said. But it was no use. I was so emotionally devastated I could barely walk.

Nikki offered a few words of encouragement and prayed with me before she hung up. My husband and the two smaller children had just left, so I was all alone in my cabin in the mountains. All alone in every way. I looked around the kitchen, strewn with the remnants of our Easter celebration: turkey leftovers, little plastic cups filled with various colored Easter-egg dyes. I collapsed on the floor in the midst of the mess.[2]

"Pick yourself up," I heard a gentle but firm voice speak to my heart.

"But I can't," I protested.

"I'll help you," he said.

I reached for the counter and slowly pulled myself up. There in front of me was an unopened package that had arrived a few days earlier. I had no idea what was inside, but I felt led to open it. It contained a cassette tape and a Post-it Note with this scribbled message: "A friend of mine asked me to send this to you. Love, Rosemary."

---

[2]This is a footnote for the detail-oriented reader. Yes, I realize that yesterday I talked about June and today I'm talking about Easter. And yes, I know that Easter comes before June. Although most of the events recorded in this book happened over the course of the past year, they are not recorded in chronological order. Rather, I am sharing events as they relate to the truth I am trying to convey. Fair enough?

Rosemary was a woman from Texas who had corresponded with me several times since teaching some of my previous Bible studies. There was no indication of *why* her friend sent me the tape—no clue *what* the tape was about—only the words, "Recorded at NASA, Houston, TX. December 1999." Intrigued, I threw it in the tape recorder and pressed *play*.

The tape featured the personal testimony of Leola Glass. As her story unfolded, it became obvious that our lives had many parallels. She had lived through similar pain and gotten through to the other side, healthy and whole. As I listened to her words, my heart was flooded with new hope and confidence.

I couldn't believe that the God of the universe reached out to me through a tape recorded at the Space Center. From outer space he reached down to strengthen and encourage me. He ordained comfort at exactly the moment I needed it. I knew then, deep within, that God was going to see me through. That no matter what else happened, no matter who else might abandon me, God would be true to his promise never to leave me or forsake me. I knew that there was nothing left to fear, because nothing could separate me from the love of God. At that moment, I savored the love God has for me.

> The Lord is my light and my salvation—
>   whom shall I fear?
> The Lord is the stronghold of my life—
>   of whom shall I be afraid?
> Though an army besiege me,
>   my heart will not fear;
> though war break out against me,
>   even then will I be confident. (Psalm 27:1, 3)

I decided to be strong and take heart. To stand firm on what I knew to be the truth, whether or not anyone on the planet ever believed me. God knew the truth; he believed in me.

Are you facing a situation that has shaken your confidence? Do you feel like the whole world has turned against you? Like an army has besieged you? Do you feel alone and abandoned? Be strong and take heart. You WILL see the goodness of the Lord in the land of the living. Stand firm on that.

Stand at the Crossroads and Look:

1. Have you ever felt (or do you currently feel) like an army has besieged you? Describe.

2. Did God reach down to you in a personal way? Describe.

3. Do you need God to reach down right now? Ask him.

4. Write out a prayer reflecting your desire to be strong and take heart.

5. What key lesson did you glean from today's study?

Truths to Stand Upon:

- Stand firm on what you know to be true, whether or not anyone else believes in you.
- God knows the truth about your circumstances; he believes in you.

Day Three

When You Need a Shelter

And Tamar lived in her brother Absalom's house, a desolate woman.

2 Samuel 13:20

Yesterday I shared how I had been running here and there looking for someone to comfort me in my distress. I also shared that God himself reached down to demonstrate his love for me through an audiocassette recorded—of all places—at the NASA Space Center in Houston. Today, I want to share with you the substance of that message.

The speaker, Leola Glass, shared the story of Tamar. It isn't pretty, so let me just sum it up.[3] Tamar was raped by her own brother. When he had finished assaulting her,

> He called his personal servant and said, "Get this woman out of here and bolt the door after her." So his servant put her out and bolted the door after her. She was wearing a richly ornamented robe, for this was the kind of garment the virgin daughters of the king wore. Tamar put ashes on her head and tore the ornamented robe she was wearing. She put her hand on her head and went away, weeping aloud as she went.
>
> Her brother Absalom said to her, "Has that Amnon, your brother, been with you? Be quiet now, my sister; he is your brother. Don't take this thing to heart." And Tamar lived in her brother Absalom's house, a desolate woman. (2 Samuel 13:17–20)

As if it wasn't bad enough to be raped by one brother, she had the added grief of another brother saying, "Let's just pretend it didn't

---

[3]If you want to read the whole sordid tale, turn to 2 Samuel 13.

happen, pretend it didn't hurt you." Classic denial. Far too often, that's what happens in families, isn't it? Women, in particular, are told to shut up and put up with abuse. And when a woman dares to speak up, she is labeled the troublemaker.

The phrase that grabbed me, however, was verse twenty where it says that Tamar *went to her brother's house—and she remained there A DESOLATE WOMAN.* God spoke to me as clearly as if he were standing in my kitchen that night:

> Donna, you have been running to your brothers (and sisters in Christ). If you run to them, you will remain a desolate woman forever. They can't help you. Don't run to your brother's house; run to MY house and I will heal you.

Although I had been *praying* to God, I had been *running* to people.

Do you pray to God but run to people? Maybe you skip right past the praying and break into a sprint? If you continue on that path, my friend, you will remain a desolate woman. You'll never find health and wholeness. You'll never be able to stand firm. The only place to run is to God. The only place to dwell is God's house, in God's presence, savoring his love.

I'm not saying that it's wrong to be in fellowship with our brothers and sisters in Christ. Of course we should. And they should want to help us. The Scripture exhorts us to "comfort those in any trouble with the comfort we ourselves have received" (2 Corinthians 1:4). However, it's a matter of expectations. If you expect them to be God for you, you'll be disappointed every time.

It's interesting to note that when I stopped running to people for answers, God started sending people to me. Just as he sent the audio-cassette that night, he prompted other people to send songs, poems, prayers, and words of encouragement. God will do the same for you. Think about this: When we seek him first and draw near to him, we are automatically nearer to those who are near to the heart of God.

So don't remain a desolate woman. When you need a shelter, run to your Father's house and savor the love he has for you.

Stand at the Crossroads and Look:

1. Have you ever experienced something as devastating as Tamar? Describe. (I know what I'm asking here is tremendously painful;

you may wish to write it in a private journal. But bringing the truth into the light is an important first step toward healing.)

2. Where did you run? What were the consequences?

3. In the daily crises of life, do you pray to God but run to people? Maybe even skip the prayer? What are the results?

4. Write out a prayer expressing your desire to receive healing and wholeness in the house of your Father.

5. What key lesson did you glean from today's study?

Truths to Stand Upon:

- If you run to your brothers and sisters in Christ, rather than seeking God first, you will remain a desolate woman.
- When we draw near to God, we are automatically nearer to those who are near to the heart of God.

Day Four

A Romantic Evening

O God, you are my God,
*   earnestly I seek you;*
my soul thirsts for you,
*   my body longs for you,*
in a dry and weary land
*   where there is no water.*   Psalm 63:1

I want you to imagine a romantic evening with an incredibly hand-some man who is madly in love with you. That shouldn't be hard to do, because most women have vivid imaginations. Too vivid, if you're anything like me! This man has gone to great lengths to pursue you. Ever since you were a little girl, he has loved you, wanted you, chased you. In high school, you spent a few wonderful weekends together. In college, you'd see him from time to time. Sometimes you'd visit him in the morning before you went to class. But you were always so busy "playing hard to get" that you never quite connected—not in the deep, intimate way you sensed he wanted to connect.

So now, the big night has arrived. You like him, too, and you've been looking forward to this time together. The stage is set. Flowers. Candlelight. Soft music playing. He gazes into your eyes and begins to speak softly.

Your cell phone rings.

Uh-oh. But you've got to take the call. It's urgent. He waits pa-tiently, but you can tell his feelings are hurt.

You finally hang up the phone and start chatting about all that's going on in your life—how your job is driving you nuts, and you need a new car, and your mom's not feeling well. He listens intently. It's hard for him to get a word in edgewise. When you come up for air, he leans forward to speak, but his voice is so quiet you can barely hear him. It makes you uncomfortable.

Then you remember! You've got just the thing for an awkward moment like this: a portable checkers game, the kind you play on a cute little cloth. So you take out the game, set it up, and get really focused on what you are doing and how well you're playing. When the game is up, you're not quite sure what to do or say next. There's another silent pause. Suddenly (thankfully) you notice your next-door neighbors coming into the restaurant! You invite them over to the table, and they decide to join you. Pretty soon, you're more focused on your friends than on your date. He leans back in his chair, watching you, still longing to draw close, but disappointed once again. Later that evening, he sits alone and cries.

How tragic. For this was the very night he wanted to tell you just how much he has always loved you. How he has longed to hold you in his arms, cherishing you, comforting you. But not now. Not like this. It's impossible to have an intimate conversation in the midst of so much chaos.

My sisters, God is the handsome man at the dinner table. He is the one who has been pursuing you all of your life. From the time you were a little girl and he whispered your name on the playground. When you were in high school and he called you away for a weekend retreat with the youth group. You met him there, and you knew he was real. He pursued you all through college, even though you only turned to him when you needed to ace a test.

And now, even now, he is the one who longs to draw you into intimate conversation. But we'll have none of it. We'd rather engage in idle chitchat, rather give him a litany of our problems, rather play dumb games. Even our quiet times, when we bother to have them, are often superficial. Like a checkers game, where we look up this verse and that verse, move here and there in our Bibles, maybe jot down a couple notes before the phone rings, or our kids come bounding down the stairs, or our mind drifts off.

God won't have an intimate conversation in the midst of chaos, no more than a romantic suitor would speak intimately while our neighbors were sitting at the table. If we would hear him express his love, his deep love for us, then we need to sit quietly, undistracted, and listen. We need to show God, the lover of our soul, the same attentive courtesy we would show an earthly lover.

I want you to prepare to go on a date with God tomorrow night. I want you to prepare yourself mentally, emotionally, and spiritually to have an intimate conversation with him. Today you can set the stage. Plan the time and place. Make it a quiet, beautiful place, the kind that is conducive to romance. Have candlelight (even if your date will be during the day), soft music, fresh flowers in a vase nearby. Take the phone off the hook. Put a "Do Not Disturb" sign on the door. Hire a baby-sitter if you need to. Put on a beautiful dress. This is a date. It's a big deal.

Be ready. God will pick you up tomorrow[4] night at _____. (You fill in the time!) It's going to be an evening to remember.

Stand at the Crossroads and Look:

1. Write your reaction to the "date."

2. How did you feel when you realized the date described was God?

3. Have your dates with God been like the one described? Have you ever had a wonderful date with God? Tell about it.

---

[4] I realize "tomorrow night" may be too short notice for some of you. That's okay. Plan to do it as soon as you possibly can. God is a gentleman; he'll schedule the date at *your* convenience.

4. Write out a prayer to God expressing your excitement about the "big date" tomorrow night.

5. What key lesson did you glean from today's study?

Truths to Stand Upon:

- God wants to have an intimate conversation with you, but he won't do it in the midst of chaos.
- We need to show God, the lover of our soul, the same attentive courtesy we would show an earthly lover.

Day Five

Your Date With God

For your Maker is your husband—
the Lord Almighty is his name.

Isaiah 54:5

Hopefully, you have set the stage, and you are ready for your date with God. Be open to his leading and listen intently for his voice. Resist the temptation to fill in all the silences. Sit quietly. Seek to gaze into his eyes. Allow your spirit to savor the love he has for you.

When I had my date with God, I played Jill Phillips' self-titled debut CD. It features the song "Steel Bars," which has been particularly meaningful to me throughout this past year. I ate my dinner slowly and tried to imagine that Jesus was sitting at the table with me. I talked out loud to him and tried to listen attentively for his voice. Afterward I sat on the couch and imagined resting my head on his shoulders while I listened to "I Am," and just cried like a baby.

Then I sensed God inviting me to slow dance with him. I was nervous, just like I was back in high school when some boy got up his nerve and walked my way. We danced to "Everyday." It was a very, very beautiful evening. I won't share everything that happened on our date. Men don't like women who kiss and tell. I'll just say it was a wonderful experience, but afterward, I worried that there was something weird or doctrinally incorrect about it. In fact, I was reluctant to include it in this book.

However, when I confided the story to one of my spiritual mentors, she recounted a similar experience she had had with God. I felt much better, because she is a well-grounded woman whom no one could accuse of being even remotely off-the-wall. (This is in contrast to me, a nutty woman who is frequently accused of being off-the-wall.) Anyway, every date is unique, so don't have a preconceived agenda. Just be ready to enjoy God.

I've included some of my favorite Scriptures for you to prayerfully consider. There is room after each passage for you to write out a prayer of response. I've also included space at the end of today's lesson for you to journal about the experience. Other than that, just relax, enjoy your date, and truly savor the love God has for you.

> "Do not be afraid; you will not suffer shame.
> Do not fear disgrace; you will not be humiliated.
> You will forget the shame of your youth
> and remember no more the reproach of your widowhood.
> For your Maker is your husband—
> the Lord Almighty is his name—
> the Holy One of Israel is your Redeemer;
> he is called the God of all the earth.
> The Lord will call you back
> as if you were a wife deserted and distressed in spirit—
> a wife who married young,
> only to be rejected," says your God. (Isaiah 54:4–6)

Respond to your husband.

But now, this is what the Lord says—
   he who created you, O Jacob,
   he who formed you, O Israel:
"Fear not, for I have redeemed you;
   I have summoned you by name; you are mine.
When you pass through the waters,
   I will be with you;
and when you pass through the rivers,
   they will not sweep over you.
When you walk through the fire,
   you will not be burned;
   the flames will not set you ablaze.
For I am the Lord, your God,
   the Holy One of Israel, your Savior;
I give Egypt for your ransom,
   Cush and Seba in your stead.
Since you are precious and honored in my sight,
   and because I love you,
I will give men in exchange for you,
   and people in exchange for your life.
Do not be afraid, for I am with you;
   I will bring your children from the east
   and gather you from the west.
I will say to the north, 'Give them up!'
   and to the south, 'Do not hold them back.'
Bring my sons from afar
   and my daughters from the ends of the earth—
everyone who is called by my name,
   whom I created for my glory,
   whom I formed and made." (Isaiah 43:1–7)

Express your love and gratitude to your Creator.

"I took you from the ends of the earth,
    from its farthest corners I called you.
I said, 'You are my servant';
    I have chosen you and have not rejected you.
So do not fear, for I am with you;
    do not be dismayed, for I am your God.
I will strengthen you and help you;
    I will uphold you with my righteous right hand.
All who rage against you
    will surely be ashamed and disgraced;
those who oppose you
    will be as nothing and perish.
Though you search for your enemies,
    you will not find them.
Those who wage war against you
    will be as nothing at all.
For I am the Lord, your God,
    who takes hold of your right hand
and says to you, Do not fear;
    I will help you." (Isaiah 41: 9–13)

Thank the God "who takes hold of your right hand."

Stand at the Crossroads and Look:

1. Journal about your date with God.

2. What key lesson did you glean from today's study?

3. Write out This Week's Verse from memory.

Truths to Stand Upon:

- Your Maker is your husband.
- You are precious and honored in God's sight.

Weekly Review:

Take a few moments to fill in the ten actions and attitudes required to Stand Firm. Look in the back of the book if you need help.

S _____ God first

S _____ God's perspective

S _____ your spiritual hunger

S _____ the love God has for you

S _____ yourself against the attacks of the enemy

S _____ truth to yourself and others

S _____ the tide of mediocrity

S _____ like a saint

S _____ wholeheartedly

S _____ firm until the end

WEEK FIVE:

Strengthen Yourself Against the Attacks of the Enemy

This Week's Verse:

Be self-controlled and alert. Your enemy the devil prowls around like a roaring lion looking for someone to devour. Resist him, standing firm in the faith, because you know that your brothers throughout the world are undergoing the same kind of sufferings.

1 Peter 5:8–9

Day One

Know Your Enemy

Be self-controlled and alert. Your enemy the devil prowls around like a roaring lion looking for someone to devour. Resist him, standing firm in the faith, because you know that your brothers throughout the world are undergoing the same kind of sufferings.

1 Peter 5:8–9

When it comes to knowing our enemy,[1] Christians tend to fall into two extreme camps: Camp #1 sees a demon under every rock and Camp #2 wouldn't know a demon if it walked up and introduced itself. I've spent time in both Camps: Obsessed and Oblivious. I hope to present a balanced perspective here. It's inconceivable for me to give fair treatment to the topic of spiritual warfare in five short lessons, so I would encourage you to read books specifically written on this topic. Nevertheless, if we would make progress toward standing firm, we need to know who our enemy is, what his objectives are, and what his final destiny is.

First, who is he?

Simply put: Satan is a fallen angel:

How you have fallen from heaven,
    O morning star, son of the dawn!
You have been cast down to the earth,
    you who once laid low the nations! (Isaiah 14:12)

---

[1]When I use the term "enemy" I am not referring to Satan personally. As we shall discover, Satan can only be in one place at a time, so the chance that he is personally attacking you at any given moment is quite remote. Instead, I am referring to that legion of fallen angels who work to advance his agenda. I refuse to capitalize "enemy" because they deserve no such distinction.

Although he clearly heads a powerful army, that still leaves the majority of the angels on God's side.

The most important thing to remember is this: Satan is not God. Nor is he "a god." As C.S. Lewis explains, ". . . some of these [angels], by the abuse of their free will, have become enemies to God and, as a corollary, to us. These we may call devils. Satan, the leader or dictator of devils, is the opposite, not of God, but of Michael [the archangel]."[2] Specifically, that means Satan is not omnipotent. Although he is certainly powerful, he is not half as powerful as some would have us believe. The book of Job clearly reveals that he must present himself before God and must obtain permission before launching attacks against God's children:

> One day the angels came to present themselves before the Lord, and Satan also came with them. The Lord said to Satan, "Where have you come from?"
>
> Satan answered the Lord, "From roaming through the earth and going back and forth in it."
>
> Then the Lord said to Satan, "Have you considered my servant Job? There is no one on earth like him; he is blameless and upright, a man who fears God and shuns evil."
>
> "Does Job fear God for nothing?" Satan replied. "Have you not put a hedge around him and his household and everything he has? You have blessed the work of his hands, so that his flocks and herds are spread throughout the land. But stretch out your hand and strike everything he has, and he will surely curse you to your face."
>
> The Lord said to Satan, "Very well, then, everything he has is in your hands, but on the man himself do not lay a finger." (Job 1:6–12)

Satan strikes at Job's family and possessions, but Job "still maintains his integrity" (Job 2:3). He stands firm. Satan then has to *ask permission* to launch another attack:

> The Lord said to Satan, "Very well, then, he is in your hands; but you must spare his life." (Job 2:6)

Clearly, God maintains sovereign control over the nature and

---

[2]*The Screwtape Letters*, by C. S. Lewis, New York, NY: Simon and Schuster, reprinted 1996, p. 6.

intensity of attacks. Jesus reiterates this in Luke 22:31–32. "Simon, Simon, Satan has asked to sift you as wheat. But I have prayed for you, Simon, that your faith may not fail. And when you have turned back, strengthen your brothers."

It's difficult to understand why God allows the enemy to attack us, but one thing is clear: He does. But he is able to redeem the fallout of the attack and turn it around for his own glory and our ultimate good. God is such an amazing Redeemer! In Peter's case, as in ours, the purpose is often that we might turn and strengthen our brothers.

Now here's more good news about this enemy of ours: He is not omniscient (all-knowing). Therefore, he can't read your thoughts, and he doesn't know every detail of your life. I will leave the more complex issue of whether or not he can *plant thoughts in your mind* to the real theologians.

Satan is not omnipresent; therefore he cannot be in more than one place at a time. So if, at any given time, two people are claiming, "the devil made me do it," one of them is obviously deceived.

Second, what are his objectives?

You said in your heart,
> "I will ascend to heaven;
I will raise my throne
> above the stars of God;
I will sit enthroned on the mount of assembly,
> on the utmost heights of the sacred mountain.
I will ascend above the tops of the clouds;
> I will make myself like the Most High."
But you are brought down to the grave,
> to the depths of the pit. (Isaiah 14:13–15)

Satan wants to be equal with God. He wants to ascend, to be lifted up, to be important. Now think about this for a moment. When we make Satan the center of our focus, when we spend half of our prayer time addressing *him* rather than our Father, we're giving him the attention he craves. When we become obsessed with his activities, we are, in essence, lifting him up. When we give him *more credit* than he deserves for what takes place in our world, we are exalting him. Don't do it.

There's an interesting scene in the movie *Out of Africa*. Karen Blixen has just arrived from Denmark and is completely clueless about life on the savannah. She is out walking, unarmed, when a lion confronts her. As she stands there, terror struck, a wise hunter happens upon her and offers this advice from shouting distance: "Don't run, Baroness, or she'll think you're something good to eat." Baroness Blixen stares the lion right in the eyes, stands her ground, and sure enough, the lion walks away.

Yes, we have an enemy roaming around like a roaring lion, actively seeking someone to devour. But if we simply stand firm in the face of his attacks, he'll go roar somewhere else. We have God's Word on that: "Resist the devil, and he WILL flee from you" (James 4:7, emphasis added). We don't need to become obsessed with him, but neither should we ignore him. We should see him for the "roaring lion" he is and respond accordingly: Don't run. Stand firm.

Third, what is his destiny?

But you are brought down to the grave,
    to the depths of the pit.
Those who see you stare at you,
    they ponder your fate:
"Is this the man who shook the earth
    and made kingdoms tremble,
the man who made the world a desert,
    who overthrew its cities
    and would not let his captives go home?" (Isaiah 14:15–17)

We would do well to remember that we are being attacked by a defeated enemy. Of course, that also makes him desperate and, therefore, very dangerous. As Revelation 12:12 reminds us, "He is filled with fury, because he knows that his time is short." Yet the day is coming when he, too, will bend the knee before our God and King. To borrow a teenage phrase, "He ain't all that."

I once heard an amusing story about Martin Luther. It is said that one night, he awoke to discover his room filled with the overwhelming presence of evil. He sat up, and there, at the foot of his bed, stood

Satan himself. Martin Luther looked at him and said, "Oh, it's only you," rolled over, and went back to sleep. While I'm not so sure about the truth of that story, I do know that Martin Luther did a masterful job of summing up everything I've tried to say today about our enemy. Read and prayerfully ponder the words to his famous hymn, "A Mighty Fortress":

A mighty fortress is our God,
A bulwark never failing;
Our helper he amid the flood
Of mortal ills prevailing.
For still our ancient foe
Doth seek to work us woe—
His craft and pow'r are great,
And, armed with cruel hate,
On earth is not his equal.
Did we in our own strength confide,
Our striving would be losing,
Were not the right man on our side,
The man of God's own choosing.
Dost ask who that may be?
Christ Jesus, it is he—
Lord Sabaoth his name,
From age to age the same,
And he must win the battle.
And tho this world, with devils filled,
Should threaten to undo us,
We will not fear, for God hath willed
His truth to triumph thru us.
The prince of darkness grim,
We tremble not for him—
His rage we can endure,
For lo, his doom is sure:
One little word shall fell him.
That Word above all earthly pow'rs,
No thanks to them, abideth;
The Spirit and the gifts are ours
Thru him who with us sideth.
Let goods and kindred go,
This mortal life also—
The body they may kill;

God's truth abideth still:
His kingdom is forever.

Stand at the Crossroads and Look:

1. Are you more inclined to "see a demon under every rock" (obsessed) or to be oblivious to Satan's activities?

2. Who is Satan?

3. What is he NOT?

4. What are his objectives?

5. Have you, in any way, been helping him achieve his objectives?

6. What is his destiny?

7. What is an appropriate response to a roaring lion?

8. Write out a prayer asking God to enable you to stand firm in the face of the enemy's attacks.

9. What key lesson did you glean from today's study?

Truths to Stand Upon:

- Christians either tend to become obsessed with Satan or remain oblivious to him.
- We should see him for the "roaring lion" he is and respond accordingly: Don't run. Stand firm.

Day Two

Know Your Position

"No weapon forged against you will prevail,
    and you will refute every tongue that accuses you.
This is the heritage of the servants of the Lord,
    and this is their vindication from me,"
    declares the Lord.   Isaiah 54:17

Satan's chief weapon is lies. Jesus said, "When he lies, he speaks his native language, for he is a liar and the father of lies" (John 8:44). Satan is many things, but he's not particularly creative. He and his legion of fallen angels have been using the same handful of lies since the creation of man. His message to Eve was basic. "God is holding out on you. You are an underprivileged child!" His objective was to sow doubt about the goodness of God, which he knew, in turn, would lead to rebellion.

Just as doubting God's goodness leads to rebellion, so *resting in the goodness of God* leads to obedience. The surest way to stand firm in the face of enemy attacks is to know our position. We are NOT underprivileged children. Repeat: *We are NOT underprivileged children.* We are sons and daughters of a gracious, loving King:

> We know that anyone born of God does not continue to sin; the one who was born of God keeps him safe, and the evil one cannot harm him. We know that we are children of God, and that the whole world is under the control of the evil one. (1 John 5:18–19)

That verse sums it up: We know who we are, but we also know where we live. We are children of God, but God has placed us in a world that is under the control of the evil one. We are only here for a season, before we go to spend eternity with our Father. During our brief stay, let's do all we can to bring glory and honor to his name.

The word Satan actually means *accuser*. We saw in the Garden that Satan *accused* God of withholding good gifts from his children. It's a lie. God is NOT holding out on us. "No good thing will he withhold" (Psalm 84:11). In the book of Revelation, Satan is called "the accuser of our brothers" (Revelation 12:10), which means he stands before God hurling accusations at his children. This is exactly what he did in the case of Job. He accused Job of being a fair-weather friend of God. Let's not dishonor God by giving Satan any basis for making such accusations. We often hear people wonder, "Can I trust God?" Perhaps a more appropriate question is, "Can God trust YOU?"

The enemy also accuses us directly. He whispers in our ears, "You are such a failure as a Christian. You're never gonna make it anyway. Why don't you just give up and take it easy?" Would you believe the little demon assigned to accuse me actually calls me by a *nickname*? It's true. He calls me *pathetic*.

For years, I had an audiotape running nonstop in my head: "Donna, you are such a pathetic piece of junk." "What a pathetic excuse for a mother!" "That was a pathetic speech." "Your books are just pathetic; you're nothing compared to so-and-so." The enemy would also tempt me to "watch" destructive mental videotapes. I would visualize myself as a boxer in the ring being pummeled mercilessly, with no chance of winning. The audience couldn't bear to watch any more and would be begging me to sit down and admit defeat. Now, that's the epitome of *pathetic*, isn't it?

Last night, he tried to tell me that my attempts at explaining spiritual warfare were pathetic. He actually had me going for a while. As always, I'm slow to catch on, but I finally figured out that these lies come straight from the pit of hell. What is the enemy accusing you of? Don't believe a word of it. The truth is:

"No weapon forged against you will prevail,
    and you will refute every tongue that accuses you.
This is the heritage of the servants of the Lord,
    and this is their vindication from me,"
    declares the Lord. (Isaiah 54:17)

None of his dark lies can survive the blinding light of truth. His weapons won't prevail; his accusations will not stand. If this was the heritage of the *servants* of the Lord, how much more are we entitled to? We, of whom Jesus said:

> "I no longer call you servants, because a servant does not know his master's business. Instead, I have called you friends, for everything that I learned from my Father I have made known to you. You did not choose me, but I chose you and appointed you to go and bear fruit—fruit that will last. Then the Father will give you whatever you ask in my name." (John 15:15–16)

The truth is, we were handpicked by God. Chosen before the foundation of the world. We ARE "all that and then some!" As Rev. Joan Milar[3] has observed, "When you understand who you really are, you will touch the world in a significant way." I've taken her words, personalized them, and made them a daily affirmation of sorts: "When I understand who I really am [in Christ], I will touch the world in a significant way."

My sisters, stand firm upon the truth! Know your position, so that you can "refute every tongue that accuses you." Following is a list of common accusations, along with the suggested refutation:

ACCUSATION	REFUTATION
The enemy will tell you:	Counter the lie with this truth:
You are a worthless piece of junk.	I am a child of God. (John1:12) God says I am precious and honored in his sight. He says he loves me. (Isaiah 43:4)
You'll never change.	I am being renewed inwardly, day-by-day. (2 Corinthians 4:16)
You'll never amount to anything.	Someday, I will be just like Jesus. (1 John 3:1–2)
Everyone hates you.	God loves me so much he has engraved me on the palms of his hands. (Isaiah 49:16)

---

[3]You'll learn more about her tomorrow.

Your life doesn't matter.	I am a minister of reconcilation. (2 Corinthians 5:18–19) God has work for me to do that he prepared in advance. (Ephesians 2:10–11)
God is disappointed in you.	God says I am dearly loved. (1 Thessalonians 1:4)
You're a complete failure as a Christian.	I am perfect and holy in God's sight. (Ephesians 4:24)
You don't fit in anywhere.	I am part of God's family, one of his chosen people. (1 Peter 2:9–10 and Ephesians 2:19)
Your head is all messed up.	I have the mind of Christ. (1 Corinthians 2:16)
You have no future.	My future is with God and it is guaranteed. (2 Corinthians 1:21)
You ought to be ashamed of yourself.	There is no condemnation for me. Jesus took away my shame. (Romans 8:1)
God is really mad at you now. He doesn't even love you anymore.	God has sworn not to be angry with me. Though the mountains be shaken and the hills be removed, yet God's love for me can never be shaken and his covenant of peace can never be removed. (Isaiah 54:9–10)
Look, God is blessing everyone but you.	God has given me every blessing. (Ephesians 1:3)
You just don't have what you need.	God has given me everything I need. (2 Peter 1:3)
You better not show your face to God.	I can approach God with boldness. (Ephesians 3:12)

You have my permission to copy this information. I encourage you to carry it with you wherever you go. If you desire to stand firm, then you must remind yourself daily of your position.

Stand at the Crossroads and Look:

1. What is Satan's chief weapon?

2. Why/how does doubting the goodness of God lead to rebellion? Have you experienced it in your own life?

3. Why/how does resting in the goodness of God lead to obedience? Have you experienced it in your own life?

4. What are the most frequent accusations the enemy hurls at you?

5. Write out a prayer in response to today's lesson.

6. What key lesson did you glean from today's study?

Truths to Stand Upon:

- Doubting the goodness of God leads to rebellion; resting in the goodness of God leads to obedience.
- We are not underprivileged children! We are beloved children of a gracious King.

Day Three

Know Your Weapons

Finally, be strong in the Lord and in his mighty power. Put on the full armor of God so that you can take your stand against the devil's schemes. For our struggle is not against flesh and blood, but against the rulers, against the authorities, against the powers of this dark world and against the spiritual forces of evil in the heavenly realms. Therefore put on the full armor of God, so that when the day of evil comes, you may be able to stand your ground, and after you have done everything, to stand.

Ephesians 6:10–13

Now I'm about to make a confession that should scare you. Having been a Christian for twenty years, having written nine Christian books, having spoken to thousands of people at churches around the country, it only recently occurred to me that "spiritual warfare" actually exists. Sure, I read Neil T. Anderson's *Victory Over the Darkness*, but trust me: The war was being waged well below my radar screen.

I was so steeped in the importance of good doctrine and right behavior—not to mention being paranoid about turning into a "religious fanatic"—that I approached the Christian life as a set of beliefs and a list of rules. I was always suspicious of people who "saw a demon under every rock." It's taken me twenty years to figure out that there is, in fact, a demon under many of those rocks.

It began with a visit to the prayer team at my friendly local Baptist church. Now, Baptists are very level-headed people, not at all inclined to see demons where none are lurking. I had been sick for years. And I do mean *years*. The frequency and the intensity of the illnesses kept getting worse. If it wasn't a strep infection in my throat, it was a sinus infection in my head. Or the flu. Or a nasty cold. Or my lungs were so infected I would be up all night coughing violently for *weeks*. Then

I'd suffer from sleep deprivation on top of everything else.

The common denominator in all these illnesses was that they made me dizzy, light-headed, and unable to think straight. Half the time, when I'd begin battling yet another sinus infection, my first thought was, "I think I'm going insane." If I had a speaking engagement, you could take it to the bank: I'd get sick a day or two before.

I thought it was stress. Or poor diet. Or bad genes.

Then one Friday night, I was staring at the ceiling, disoriented and weak, in yet another hotel room. An audience was already gathering downstairs, and I literally couldn't lift my head from the pillow. And right then and there it hit me: *This is WAR.* My battle wasn't against flesh and blood. Not even my *own* flesh and blood. It was "against spiritual forces of evil in the heavenly realms."

Somehow, God enabled me to get up. I tracked down my doctor by phone and managed to convince him to call in yet another round of antibiotics to yet another pharmacy in yet another city. Even he sensed something was seriously wrong and told me he couldn't keep writing prescriptions. He said I needed to get to the root cause.

I somehow muddled through the weekend. When Thursday morning Bible study rolled around, I skipped my usual class and walked into the "Emergency Prayer Room" instead. I told the women I was sick and needed prayer. I told them nothing else. We began to pray, and they quickly concluded that I was not sick. I was under spiritual attack. Over the course of the next hour, three different women identified three specific areas of attack: a spirit of affliction against my body, chaos and confusion against my mind and my circumstances, and a spirit of rebellion in the lives of my children.

The women prayed deep, heartfelt prayers, but I think everyone in the room sensed we were in over our heads. I began to pray that God would lead me to people who could pray effectively for my deliverance, people who knew how to wield the weapons of spiritual warfare in powerful ways.

In April, I was speaking at the Ohio District Assembly of God conference in Toledo, Ohio. The other keynote speaker was Rev. Joan Milar, from Guyana, South America, who now directs the New Orleans School of Urban Missions. She gave a powerful talk, then began to conduct a healing service. Although I already admired her because of the conversation we had had during dinner earlier in the evening and because I was impressed with the depth of her biblical insight, I was extremely skeptical. I had seen televangelistic healing services. I had also seen the newsmagazine exposés revealing how phony some of these guys were. (You know, the old "miracle" where they extend someone's leg. Wink. Wink.)

Besides, the whole thing was way outside my theological comfort zone. I figured if God wanted to heal me, he would send a smart doctor to give me the right medicine. But I had a smart doctor, and he had given me a truckload of the right medicine. And I was still constantly sick. I was desperate.

I went forward for healing that night. And I have not been sick one day since. No, not one day.[4] That's not to say I won't ever get sick again.[5] I'm sure I will. In fact, I'll probably get so sick someday, I'll die from it. Then again, maybe I'll die peacefully in my sleep at the age of 106. Who knows?

I do know this: I was under attack by a spirit of affliction. It was real and it was powerful. And this sister in Christ effectively fought that spirit off. The weapons she fought with were not the weapons of this world. They had divine power.

I recognize that I'm leaping into a theological minefield here. But if I can help one person, I must speak. Okay, here goes. If you are constantly sick, is it possible you are under spiritual attack? Is someone in your family almost always sick? If it's not you, then your daughter has an earache or your son's got the flu? Is it possible that a spirit of affliction is attacking your family? Notice I did not say "there must be some sin in your life" as if there's a person on earth who *doesn't* have sin in her life. HELLO! Notice I did not say "God never allows sickness; he wants all of us to be healthy and wealthy 24/7." Notice I didn't say, "You never need a doctor. Just pray about it."

What I am saying is, "Let's open our eyes to the spiritual dimension." Life on earth is not a church picnic; it's a WAR. Church is not a social club (well, at least it's not *supposed* to be); it's the front line

---

[4]Six months and counting. Praise God!

[5]This footnote was added several months later. Get ready for this one; it's a zinger. The day after I originally wrote today's study, I woke up so ill I could barely lift my head from the pillow. I subsequently contracted a viral infection that lasted for three months, with my fever raging as high as 104 degrees. I have no idea what to make of all this. Have a ball discussing it amongst yourselves! Like I said, I don't have a theological ax to grind. I'm just sharing my life journey.

of a supernatural battle. *You have an enemy.* You can pretend you don't, but that won't shield you from attack. It will make it worse. Working harder for the Kingdom is no guarantee of protection, either. In fact, the more God begins to use you in the lives of others, the more you'll become a target for the enemy. And let's face it, if you can't lift your head off the pillow, you're not much of a threat to his cause.

Think about it. Pray about it. Then pick up your weapons and fight back. If you don't know how to wield the weapons of warfare, find someone who does. Meanwhile, "study to show yourself approved, a workman who doesn't need to be ashamed and who correctly handles the word of truth" (2 Timothy 2:15).

My saga continues. Now my health had been restored, but my world was still absolutely chaotic and my children were still driving me up the wall, being rebellious about nonsensical stuff like brushing their teeth. I kept praying that God would send another prayer warrior who could assist me as I wrestled "not against flesh and blood, but against the rulers, against the authorities, against the powers of this dark world, and against the spiritual forces of evil in the heavenly realms."

In August, I was speaking at the Philadelphia Christian Writer's Conference, which was being held on the very college campus[6] where I had met my husband twenty years earlier. I knew it would be an emotional time for me. (Those of you who've read my previous books will understand why; the rest of you will find out soon enough.) Around 10:00 P.M. the evening before my keynote talk, I felt God prompting me to get up and rewrite my speech. Not wanting to disturb my roommate, who was already sleeping, I went out into the hallway. There was another woman sitting there, reading her Bible.

After some time had passed, she approached me and said, "This may sound weird, but I believe God wants me to pray with you." I didn't even know this woman! I didn't tell her anything at all about my circumstances. She simply began to pray. Within minutes, she

---

[6]For the truly curious among you, it was a secular college. It was an absolute miracle that they let us hold a Christian conference there in the first place. I recently received an e-mail from the conference director, Marlene Bagnull, mentioning that the college has declined to host the conference in the future. The coincidences are too much to credit to fate or circumstance; God has his hands in everything!

uttered the word *confusion*. She paused and said, "You are being attacked by a spirit of confusion and a spirit of chaos." I just looked at her in stunned silence. Then asked, "How did you know that?" She said God had shown her, and she proceeded to pray with me for nearly four hours. I should say, she proceeded to wage battle "against the rulers, against the authorities, against the powers of this dark world, and against the spiritual forces of evil in the heavenly realms." I had never experienced anything like it before, but again, what happened was powerful, real, *and way out of my theological comfort zone*. This woman, C. Hope Flinchbaugh,[7] knew the *name* of someone I have lived in fear of for most of my adult life. I had never mentioned the incident to anyone; no one even knew what had happened to me. She *knew*.

By the time we finished praying, I felt so free, it was like floating on air. I could not believe the work of healing God had accomplished, or where and how he had accomplished it. It was absolutely awesome.

Okay, I know this was a long reading. It took me a long time to write it. I struggled with how to share this material, because these experiences are all new to me, and they may be new to you, as well. Although I'm no expert on spiritual warfare, at least I'm finally awake and alert to the reality that there *is* a war going on, and I'm using my weapons to fight back to the very best of my ability. I hope you can say the same.

Stand at the Crossroads and Look:

1. Are you inclined to see the Christian life as "a set of beliefs and a list of rules" rather than as a war?

---

[7] Thank you, Hope. I will never, ever forget you, my sister!

2. Respond to my recent spiritual warfare experiences. What do you think?!

3. Have you had experiences with spiritual warfare? Describe.

4. Write out a prayer asking God to give you a balanced understanding of/approach to spiritual warfare.

5. What key lesson did you glean from today's study?

Truths to Stand Upon:

- The Christian life is more than "a set of beliefs and a list of rules."
- The church isn't a social club; it's the front line in a war.

Day Four

Know Your Weapons, Part Two

Finally, be strong in the Lord and in his mighty power. Put on the full armor of God so that you can take your stand against the devil's schemes. For our struggle is not against flesh and blood, but against the rulers, against the authorities, against the powers of this dark world and against the spiritual forces of evil in the heavenly realms. Therefore put on the full armor of God, so that when the day of evil comes, you may be able to stand your ground, and after you have done everything, to stand. Stand firm then, with the belt of truth buckled around your waist, with the breastplate of righteousness in place, and with your feet fitted with the readiness that comes from the gospel of peace. In addition to all this, take up the shield of faith, with which you can extinguish all the flaming arrows of the evil one. Take the helmet of salvation and the sword of the Spirit, which is the word of God. And pray in the Spirit on all occasions with all kinds of prayers and requests. With this in mind, be alert and always keep on praying for all the saints.

Ephesians 6:10–18

As we have already seen, we are not waging battle against flesh and blood, but against spiritual powers of wickedness. Therefore, it makes perfect sense that "the weapons we fight with are not the weapons of the world. On the contrary, they have divine power to demolish strongholds" (2 Corinthians 10:4). So what exactly is a stronghold? Essentially, it is a demonically induced pattern of lies that we routinely buy into, or which are so entrenched in our mind, they've become foundational to our way of thinking, believing, and acting.

Since a stronghold is fabricated with lies, the only way to demolish it is with truth. In order to stand firm, we must allow our knowledge of God to have preeminence. We must make a conscious decision to "take captive every thought to make it obedient to Christ" (2 Corinthians 10:5).

The weapons of our warfare are outlined in Ephesians 6:10–18. I'm sure you've read this passage many times, but please carefully read it again:

> Finally, be strong in the Lord and in his mighty power. Put on the full armor of God so that you can take your stand against the devil's schemes. For our struggle is not against flesh and blood, but against the rulers, against the authorities, against the powers of this dark world and against the spiritual forces of evil in the heavenly realms. Therefore put on the full armor of God, so that when the day of evil comes, you may be able to stand your ground, and after you have done everything, to stand. Stand firm then, with the belt of truth buckled around your waist, with the breastplate of righteousness in place, and with your feet fitted with the readiness that comes from the gospel of peace. In addition to all this, take up the shield of faith, with which you can extinguish all the flaming arrows of the evil one. Take the helmet of salvation and the sword of the Spirit, which is the word of God. And pray in the Spirit on all occasions with all kinds of prayers and requests. With this in mind, be alert and always keep on praying for all the saints.

I won't do a piece-by-piece discussion of the armor; I believe it is fairly self-explanatory. You'll notice, of course, that the armor primarily provides a *defense* against attacks. The only exception, the only *offensive weapon* listed, is the Word of God. Although not specifically identified as a piece of armor, it's obvious from the passage that our other weapon is prayer.

What I would like to suggest (and this is by no means a novel idea) is to combine the two. How? By praying the Word of God. I'm always alarmed when I hear wimpy prayers. Stuff like "Oh God, please do what you already know you're gonna do because you know what's best and we don't know what's best and you do. Amen."

We should make God's Word central to our prayer life. This past week, I was blessed to receive an e-mail prayer in which the writer did a masterful job of praying Scripture on my behalf. Watch and learn!

Dear Heavenly Father,

I praise your holy, holy name. I thank you that you are a husband to Donna and a father to her children. I come humbly before your throne of grace on behalf of this family and Donna's ministry. You are her Rock, her shield, her defender. I claim Isaiah 54:17 for her: No weapon that is formed against Donna and her family shall prosper; And every tongue that accuses her and her family in judgment you will condemn. This is the heritage of Donna and her daughters, servants of the Lord. And their vindication is from you, Lord.

I also claim Isaiah 49:25 for Donna and her daughters. You have said, "For I will contend with the one who contends with Donna and her daughters." I thank you in advance for victory. The final chapter is already written, and Satan lost a long time ago. I thank you, God, for sending your angels to be in front of, behind, and on either side of Donna and her children. In Jesus' precious name and blood I pray. Amen.

Love & Prayers,
Yvonne

Wow! If that doesn't bless your socks off, I don't know what will. Here's a woman who knows how to pray effectively *because she knows God's Word*. If we don't know God's Word, then we need to learn it so that we might pray effectively as well. We would be wise to memorize various passages that we can use in our prayer times. However, I fear that relying only on short, memorized passages might prove problematic. It's sobering to remember that when Satan came to tempt Jesus, he quoted Scripture (Luke 4:1–13). However, *he quoted it out of context*. Jesus was able to refute with Scripture by quoting it *in context*.

Until you have memorized a significant number of long Scripture passages (the length keeps us mindful of the context), I think it best to pray Scripture with a Bible in hand or with a handbook of Scripture prayers, such as *The Power of a Praying Parent* and *The Power of a Praying Wife*, both by Stormie Omartian. Lee Roberts also has a series of guides, *Praying God's Will for My Husband, Praying God's Will for My Son*, and *Praying God's Will for My Daughter*.

Yesterday, I mentioned that God used a series of prayer encounters to plainly reveal the areas in which I was under attack. He then led me to people who could help me pray effectively, enabling me to experience dramatic and immediate progress. God has shown me that the final battleground must be approached differently. It will be a daily, moment-by-moment conflict; it will be trench warfare. That battleground is the spirit of rebellion in my children.

I have to remind myself daily that "I wrestle not with flesh and blood." Not even with my children's flesh and blood. My children are not the enemy, although sometimes it sure seems like they are waging war against me. They are being attacked by the enemy, by "the spiritual forces of evil in the heavenly realms."

The primary weapons I have chosen to wage this battle are *The Power of a Praying Parent*, *Praying God's Will for My Daughter*, and *The Prayer of Jabez* by Bruce Wilkinson. I have only one parenting strategy: praying for and *with* my children.

The moment my children wake up, I take them in my arms and pray with them. We pray before breakfast. No, I mean we really pray. Not just "bless the grub." We pray again before lunch and dinner. I pray with them before they go to sleep. We pray throughout the day.

Let me ask you something: If you were standing in the kitchen and offhandedly said to your children, "You know, we really need to pray for Gayle." What would happen? Anything?

I said that very sentence some time ago, as my then nine-year-old daughter was carrying dirty dishes from the table to the sink. She stopped dead in her tracks, bowed her head, and prayed on the spot. I get the same reaction from my four year old. If I mention a prayer need, she gets down to business. She doesn't "add it to her prayer list." She doesn't "promise" to pray. She prays. Immediately. Passionately. I'm telling you, these children are already prayer warriors.

Like the Scripture says, "A little child will lead them" (Isaiah 11:6). So let's follow their lead. Let's stop *talking about* prayer and start *praying*!

Stand at the Crossroads and Look:

1. What is a stronghold?

2. Are you aware of any strongholds in your own life?

3. What are the two weapons we can use to demolish strongholds?

4. Write out a Scripture prayer.

5. What key lesson did you glean from today's study?

Truths to Stand Upon:

- A stronghold is a demonically induced pattern of lies.
- Since a stronghold is fabricated with lies, the only way to demolish it is with truth.

Day Five

Wielding Your Weapons

The weapons we fight with are not the weapons of the world. On the contrary, they have divine power to demolish strongholds. We demolish arguments and every pretension that sets itself up against the knowledge of God, and we take captive every thought to make it obedient to Christ.

2 Corinthians 10:4–5

We've had enough teaching for one week! Today, let's implement what we've learned. I want you to take some time, right now, to pray these Scriptures for your children, yourself, or anyone God places on your heart. Just fill in the appropriate name:

From Psalm 1:
Dear Heavenly Father,
I pray today for _____.
May s/he be blessed.
Let _____ not walk in the counsel of the wicked
or stand in the way of sinners.
Keep _____ from sitting in the seat of mockers.
May _____ always delight in the law of the Lord,
let him/her meditate on it day and night.
Let _____ be like a tree planted by streams of water,
which yields its fruit in season.
Do not let his/her leaf wither.
May whatever _____ does prosper.
   Amen.

From Psalm 25:
To you, O Lord, I lift up _____'s soul;
in you I trust, O my God.
Do not let _____ be put to shame,

nor let _____'s enemies triumph over him/her.
No one whose hope is in you
will ever be put to shame,
but they will be put to shame
who are treacherous without excuse.
Show _____ your ways, O Lord,
teach _____ your paths;
guide _____ in your truth and teach _____,
for you are God his/her Savior.
May _____'s hope be in you all day long.
Remember, O Lord, your great mercy and love,
for they are from of old.
Remember not the sins of _____'s youth
and _____'s rebellious ways;
according to your love remember _____,
for you are good, O Lord.
Lord, you are good and upright;
therefore instruct _____ in your ways.
Guide _____ in what is right
and teach _____ your way.
Lord, all your ways are loving and faithful
for those who keep the demands of your covenant.
For the sake of your name, O Lord,
forgive _____'s iniquity, though it is great.
Let _____ be known as one who fears the Lord.
Instruct _____ in the way chosen for him/her.
May _____ spend his/her days in prosperity,
and may _____'s descendants inherit the land.
Lord, you confide in those who fear you;
Let _____ be one of them.
Make your covenant known to _____.
Let _____'s eyes be ever on you, Lord,
for only you can release _____'s feet from the snare.
Turn to _____ and be gracious to _____,
for _____ is lonely and afflicted.
The troubles of _____'s heart have multiplied;
free _____ from anguish.
Look upon _____'s affliction and distress
and take away all _____'s sins.
See how _____'s enemies have increased
and how fiercely they hate _____!

Guard _____'s life and rescue him/her;
Do not let _____ be put to shame,
Instead, urge _____ to take refuge in you.
May integrity and uprightness protect _____,
because his/her hope is in you.
    O God, Redeem _____ from all his/her troubles!

From Psalm 91:
Most High God, I pray that _____ would always dwell in
    your shelter,
that _____ will rest in the shadow of the Almighty.
Enable _____ to know and believe that You are his/her
    refuge and fortress,
His/her God, in whom s/he can always trust.
Save _____ from the fowler's snare
and from the deadly pestilence.
Cover _____ with your feathers,
Let _____ find refuge under your wings;
Let your faithfulness be _____'s shield and rampart.
Do not let _____ fear the terror of night,
nor the arrow that flies by day,
nor the pestilence that stalks in the darkness,
nor the plague that destroys at midday.
Even if a thousand fall at _____'s side,
ten thousand at _____'s right hand,
let it not come near _____.
Let _____ observe with his/her eyes
and see the punishment of the wicked.
Most High God, I pray that _____ will make you his/her
    dwelling—
be _____'s refuge—
then no harm will befall _____,
no disaster will come near _____'s tent.
Command your angels concerning _____
to guard _____ in all his/her ways;
Let your angels lift _____ up in their hands,
so that _____ will not strike his/her foot against a stone.
Enable _____ to tread upon the lion and the cobra;
let _____ trample the great lion and the serpent.
Because _____ loves you, please rescue him/her;
Protect _____ for s/he acknowledges your name.

May _____ call upon you, and be faithful to answer.
Be with _____ in trouble,
Deliver _____ and honor _____.
Satisfy _____ with long life
and show _____ your salvation.

From Joshua 1:
Father, I pray that you would empower _____ to be strong and courageous. May _____ lead his/her children to inherit the land you have promised to give them. [Grant him/her the blessing of a godly dynasty.] May _____ always be careful to obey the truths I am teaching him/her through your Word. Do not let _____ turn from it to the right or to the left, that s/he may be successful wherever s/he goes. Do not let this Book of the Law depart from _____'s mouth; Remind him/her to meditate on it day and night, so that s/he may be careful to do everything written in it. Lord, I pray that you would make _____ prosperous and successful. Let _____ be strong and courageous. Do not let _____ be terrified; do not let her give way to discouragement. Remind _____ daily that you are his/her God, and you will be with him/her wherever s/he goes.

I recently read Bruce Wilkinson's book *The Prayer of Jabez*, which I highly recommend. In it, he suggests a pattern of prayer based on 1 Chronicles 4. I have adapted it and use it as my morning prayer for my children. As I hold them, I place my hand on their heads or simply rock them and pray aloud:

Lord, I pray that you would bless _____.
Expand her territory, Father. Let her life have a broad, far-reaching
    impact for your Kingdom.
Let your hand always be strong upon her. Let her feel your pres-
    ence.
Keep her safe from evil deeds and bad people, bad choices that
    would lead her astray.
Amen.

Well, I think that's enough to get you started. You know your enemy, you know your position, you know your weapons, and now you know how to use them. Praise God!

Stand at the Crossroads and Look:

1. Your assignment today is to pray through the Scriptures listed, then search your Bible, select a passage, and write your own Scripture prayer below.

2. Write out This Week's Verse from memory.

Truths to Stand Upon:

- The primary weapons of our warfare are the Word of God and prayer.
- The most effective prayers we can offer on behalf of our loved ones are those taken directly from the pages of Scripture.

Weekly Review

Take a few moments to fill in the ten actions and attitudes required to Stand Firm. Look in the back of the book if you need help.

S _____ God first

S _____ God's perspective

S _____ your spiritual hunger

S _____ the love God has for you

S _____ yourself against the attacks of the enemy

S _____ truth to yourself and others

S _____ the tide of mediocrity

S _____ like a saint

S _____ wholeheartedly

S _____ firm until the end

WEEK SIX:

Speak Truth to Yourself and Others

This Week's Verse:

"My prayer is not that you take them out of the world
but that you protect them from the evil one.
They are not of the world, even as I am not of it.
Sanctify them by the truth; your word is truth."

John 17:15–17

Day One

Know the Truth

"I am coming to you now, but I say these things while I am still in the world, so that they may have the full measure of my joy within them. I have given them your word and the world has hated them, for they are not of the world any more than I am of the world. My prayer is not that you take them out of the world but that you protect them from the evil one. They are not of the world, even as I am not of it. Sanctify them by the truth; your word is truth. As you sent me into the world, I have sent them into the world. For them I sanctify myself, that they too may be truly sanctified."

John 17:13–19

You're not gonna believe this one! After I finished writing last week's lessons, I felt completely drained. I decided to go work out at the gym, just to get the blood pumping again. On the way home, I checked the mailbox and found the following letter waiting. Enjoy some excerpts:

The thought that keeps coming to me as I pray for you and yours is: Tell Donna to try not to allow thoughts of the devil to [consume] her mind, and dwell only on thoughts of God and the heaped-up, overflowing love, *power*, and blessings coming down from the Three-in-One.

Fear is not of God . . . but a tool of the devil. If we allow thoughts of the devil to occupy our mind, then we are allowing power to the devil. I don't believe we are to put our head in the sand, but try hard to give *all* our thoughts to God.

I shall pray that you can visualize yourself and all of your loved ones in the palm of God's huge hand, surrounded by His power and love.

My love to you,
Elaine Doubrava

Talk about a word in due season! We spent an entire week thinking about the enemy. We've taken our heads out of the proverbial sand. Now, however, it's time to refocus our attention on the Three-in-One.

Jesus said he deliberately left us in this world, and his goal for our time here is that we would be "sanctified by the truth." Sanctified by God's Word. Sanctify is from the Greek word *hagiazo*, meaning "set apart for sacred use" or "made holy." God's purpose in leaving a holy remnant on the earth is that we might be for his sacred use, that we might be vessels of his mercy in a fallen world.

In order that we might fulfill that purpose, it's vital that we know the truth. Specifically, especially in view of what we discovered last week, we must make it a habit not only to *know* the truth, but also to *speak the truth to ourselves and others*. But we can't speak it if we don't know it. That's why I feel so passionately about studying and *memorizing* God's Word. (You *have* been keeping up with your memory verses, haven't you?)

I must make a confession: I have fallen in love. Not with a man. With a software program. It's a Scripture memory tool called PCMemlok.[1] Here's how it works: Every time I turn on my computer, PCMemlok is programmed to automatically pop up on the screen. It presents a series of verses which I am currently memorizing. You can select from thousands of verses, listed by the book or by topic. The timer is automatically set for five minutes of daily review. Is five minutes a big deal? I don't think so. But you would be amazed what a difference it makes. (You can adjust the program to run for ten minutes or more, if you like!)

For those of you who don't have a computer, there's another system I've been using simultaneously. At the beginning of the summer, I purchased a spiral-bound packet of fifty ruled index cards (available at Wal-Mart and other stationery stores). Then each week, as our Bible study teacher[2] assigned a new memory verse, I wrote it on one of the index cards. (By the way, what's up with taking summers off

---

[1]To order, call PCMemlok at 1-800-373-1947. Download a demo at www.memlok.com. The cost is only $59.00. Be sure to tell Drake I said, "Hi." He'll get a big kick out of it!

[2]I'm indebted to my teacher, Kathleen McQuain, for the spiral index card idea. She said she got it from someone else. Pass it along! By the way, most of the women in our group decorated their covers. I never got around to it.

from Bible study? We continue year-round. Sure, people have to miss because of vacations, so what? Press on!) The other women in the group, who had already completed *Walking in Total God-Confidence*, had taped their perforated verse cards into the index card packet as well. Throughout the summer, I carried my index cards with me wherever I went. Hey, I even had to buy a new purse, because my old one was too tiny to contain the bundle of wisdom. I, who hate big purses!!! See what sacrifices I'm making for my spiritual growth?

It was worth it! In addition to Scripture verses assigned by our teacher, I jotted down Scriptures I discovered on my own. I also kept a running list of verses other people mentioned, so I could look them up at my leisure. I included quotes, poems, and key points from sermons I heard.

I also took notes from books that I was reading. In other words, I created bullet points like those I provide to you each day. This is a wonderful discipline that I would encourage you to develop. When you're reading a book, glean the key points, write them down, and review them. Too often, we read with idle minds. Or even if we pay attention at the moment, we walk away and quickly forget what we learned. Write it down, and the truth you've discovered will be more likely to stay with you.

The beauty of the index cards is that you take them with you *everywhere*. Waiting in a bank line? Take out the cards! Sitting at the doctor's office? Take out the cards! Picking your kids up from school? Take out the cards! Sitting at the kitchen table? Take out the cards! Commercial time during your favorite show? Take out the cards! Okay, I think you've got the idea. Listen, don't tell me you can't memorize Scripture unless you have worked on it for at least ten minutes a day, every day, for a year. Then if you still claim you can't do it, I'll listen to you.

By the end of the summer, I had filled my index card notebook. It was so awesome to look back and remember all the truths God had shown me. It was not only a wonderful tool, now it serves as a compact diary of that season of my faith journey. When I sat down to write this book, my *first step* was to take out my index cards. I was able to quickly outline the entire book, just from those fifty cards. The verses you are memorizing are the verses I had written there. The stories I am telling you are the stories I had noted there. Who knows how God will use *your* index cards in the future? Maybe you'll write a book. Or teach a class. Or touch just one life. God knows!

The other thing I'm crazy over is Post-it Notes. I've confessed in previous books that my house looks like it's been overrun by an army of Post-it Notes. I jot verses on them and stick 'em everywhere. The two most popular spots are: above the kitchen sink and straight in front of the toilet seat, eye level. I'm speaking the truth here!

Okay, finish today's homework, then get on over to Wal-Mart. Insider's tip: Resist the temptation to get the jazzy fluorescent, multi-color pack. Stick with the boring white index cards, or you'll end up straining your eyesight. (Our class learned that the hard way!)

Stand at the Crossroads and Look:

1. Today's assignment: Go buy your index card notebook. You can tape your perforated verse cards into it, or rewrite them onto the cards.

2. Write out a prayer expressing your desire to know God's Word more fully.

3. What key lesson did you glean from today's study?

Truths to Stand Upon:

- God's purpose in leaving a holy remnant on the earth is that we might be for his sacred use, that we might be vessels of his mercy in a fallen world.
- In order that we might fulfill that purpose, it's vital that we know the truth.

Day Two

The Overflow of the Heart

"For out of the overflow of the heart the mouth speaks. The good man brings good things out of the good stored up in him, and the evil man brings evil things out of the evil stored up in him. But I tell you that men will have to give account on the day of judgment for every careless word they have spoken. For by your words you will be acquitted, and by your words you will be condemned."

Matthew 12:34–37

Words are powerful. God spoke a word, and the world came into existence. The book of John tells us, "In the beginning was the Word, and the Word was with God, and the Word was God. He was with God in the beginning. Through him all things were made; without him nothing was made that has been made" (John 1:1–3). Jesus spoke a word and people were healed.

God says our words are so important, that we will have to give an account *for every one of them*. Yet if you're anything like me, you often don't even listen to yourself. It's not until your words are "thrown back in your face" that you realize the damage you have done. Our children's pastor recently used a powerful illustration in his mini-sermon. He handed out a bunch of spoons to the kids gathered at the front of the church. Then he took a tube of toothpaste and squeezed out the contents onto a table. "Okay, kids," he said, "put all the toothpaste back in." Of course, they couldn't. And when they tried, they made an even bigger mess! He said that toothpaste is just like the words that flow from our lips. Once they go out, we can't put them back again. Often when we try to "take them back," we make a bigger mess.

Sound familiar?

I used to play this little game where I would see how long I could keep my mouth shut. Actually, I shouldn't say "used to." I played it just this week! Sure enough, when I couldn't hold my tongue a minute longer, I opened my mouth and *immediately* got myself into trouble. No kidding! I always seem to say just the wrong thing. Several years ago, I went so far as to take the Dale Carnegie course on "How to Win Friends and Influence People" by always saying the right thing. I honestly thought the class would help. It didn't. In fact, I couldn't even win friends among my classmates!

See, the problem doesn't start with my mouth. It starts with my heart and mind. My heart and mind have been corrupted by lies, chief among them being, "No one likes you, so you may as well give them a reason not to like you. Quick, say something stupid. That way, when you realize no one likes you, you can understand why." I expect to be rejected; so I act in a way that inspires rejection. I'm still battling to break free from these lies! (Excuse me while I practice: I do not deserve to be rejected. I am a Princess! A daughter of the King. I am a blessing to everyone who meets me!)

The key to changing my mouth is changing my heart and mind. The key is speaking the truth to myself. William Backus, author of *Telling Yourself the Truth*, explains it this way: "Human emotion is determined by what we think. The way we think determines who we are. When we replace lies with the truth, we will be able to live a rich and fulfilling emotional life."[3]

This book was the first tool God used to open my eyes to the truth that negative, distorted, repeated statements come from the devil himself.[4] We talked about that last week. The point I want to make today is that these lies become part of the fabric of our being. They become "misbeliefs" that shape the way we feel about ourselves, which leads to negative behaviors, which results in negative reactions from people, which strengthens the lie and increases our negative feelings. And on and on and on.

I have lived this pattern all my life. And I know the only way I'm ever going to break free is to begin speaking the truth. Out loud. To myself and to anyone who will listen. Are you listening? Have you been believing lies? Remember: Any negative, distorted, repeated statement originates with the enemy. Once the thoughts are planted, of course, they begin to take on a life of their own. To use our term

---

[3]Bethany House Publishers, 1980, p. 16.
[4]Backus, p. 18.

from last week, they become a stronghold.

Backus goes on to explain that if you believe something, you obviously act like you believe it and it becomes a self-fulfilling prophecy. If you think something awful is going to happen, it usually does. It's like waking up and saying to yourself over and over again, "Today, I'm going to see a blue Volvo." Your subconscious mind sets to work, and you can bet it won't rest *until it sees a blue Volvo.*

What are you asking your subconscious mind to look for today? You can bet it won't rest until it finds it! You can choose to look for negative, depressing stuff . . . and you'll surely find it. Or you can choose to look for positive, uplifting stuff . . . and you'll surely find it. Many of us are caught in downward emotional spirals because we are constantly looking for—and finding—what's wrong with the world, rather than what's right with it. I know whereof I speak, my friend.

Backus goes so far as to assert that "your beliefs are the most important factor in your mental health. Misbeliefs are the direct cause of emotional turmoil, maladaptive behavior and mental illness."[5] I'm no expert in the field of psychology, but one truth I'm now absolutely convinced of—and this certainly lines up with Scripture—is that our thoughts affect our biochemistry, just as much as our biochemistry affects our thoughts. That's why the Scripture exhorts us to think positive:[6]

> Finally, brothers, whatever is true, whatever is noble, whatever is right, whatever is pure, whatever is lovely, whatever is admirable—if anything is excellent or praiseworthy—think about such things. Whatever you have learned or received or heard from me, or seen in me—put it into practice. And the God of peace will be with you. (Philippians 4:8–9)

Did you notice the last line? When we speak the truth and meditate on all the wonderful things God has done, then we enjoy the *peace* of God. And what is peace if not the *opposite* of emotional turmoil?

Some time ago, I was on the phone giving a friend a litany of my

---

[5]Backus, p. 17.
[6]I need to state a caveat here. I think the "power of positive thinking" and "positive confession" have been abused. Nevertheless, when kept in balance, they are important, scriptural teachings.

woes. She listened compassionately for a while, then lovingly rebuked me: "Donna, you need to count your blessings, girl." A few days later, another friend sent me the following e-mail. It's filled with solid truths we need to remind ourselves of daily:

You Are Blessed

If you woke up this morning with more health than illness, you are more blessed than the 1,000,000 people who will not survive the week.

If you have never experienced the danger of battle, the loneliness of imprisonment, the agony of torture, or the pangs of starvation, you are more blessed than 500 million people around the world.

If you attend a church meeting without fear of harassment, arrest, torture, or death, you are more blessed than 3 billion people in the world.

If you have food in your refrigerator, clothes on your back, a roof over your head, and a place to sleep, you are richer than 75 percent of this world.

If you have money in the bank, in your wallet, and spare change in a dish somewhere, you are among the top 8 percent of the world's wealthy.

If you can read this message, you are more blessed than 2 billion people in the world who cannot read anything at all.

If you hold up your head with a smile on your face and are truly thankful, you are blessed because the majority can, but most do not.

Stand at the Crossroads and Look:

1. What do you tell your mind to look for when you wake up in the morning?

2. Do you tend to look for the positive or the negative? What is the result?

3. Have you experienced the pattern described today? (Negative beliefs lead to negative behaviors, which lead to negative reactions, which reinforce the negative beliefs). Explain how you've seen this dynamic at work in your life.

4. What are some practical ways you can begin to break free from that negative pattern?

5. Respond to the truths contained in "You Are Blessed."

6. Write out a prayer of thanksgiving to God.

7. What key lesson did you glean from today's study?

Truths to Stand Upon:

- Our mind will find whatever we tell it to look for, whether positive or negative.
- Many of us are caught in downward emotional spirals because we are constantly looking for—and finding—what's wrong with the world, rather than what's right with it.

Day Three

Give Away the Truth

Pay attention and listen to the sayings of the wise;
*   apply your heart to what I teach,*
for it is pleasing when you keep them in your heart
*   and have all of them ready on your lips.*

Proverbs 22:17–18

God says he is pleased, not only when we study his Word and store it in our own hearts, but also when we "have all of them ready on our lips." When we get into the habit of speaking the truth to ourselves, we will be better equipped to speak truth to others. Of course, it works both ways: I've discovered the very best way to learn a truth is to share it with someone else. That's why I keep writing these books, you know. It forces me to keep learning and growing, so that I'll have something to share with you.

As a simple illustration, when I'm memorizing a verse, I share it as often as I can. If I'm ending a phone conversation with someone, I might suggest we pray together—and I'll use that Scripture to close. I might write a note card to someone—and include that Scripture. Or I might e-mail a friend—and mention the Scripture. The same thing goes for new truths God shows me in his Word. I seem to remember them better when I immediately tell someone else what I've just learned. Or when I'm reading a book, I'll weave a discussion of it into conversations with people. It's a scientifically proven fact that the simple act of putting something you've learned into your own words seals the truth to your mind. It forces you to process and synthesize the information in such a way that it actually goes into a deeper part of your brain. When you go beyond sharing what you've learned to ac-tually *applying* it to a specific situation, it is even more firmly planted in your mind. (I'm no expert on brain structure, but that's the gist of things!)

Once again, I'd like to share an e-mail I received along these lines. I realize how dangerous this is because you're all gonna e-mail me your spiritual insights in hopes of being in my next book. Well, go ahead! You can speak the truth to me *anytime*! Here goes:

Dear Donna,

As I was praying for you this morning, I was impressed to send you this message. A while ago a close friend of mine—a woman who walks close to the Lord—and I both separately saw this truth at the same time. When we shared it with each other, it was as if God put a big exclamation point after it. I believe it applies to your situation.

You know the story of Shadrach, Meshach, and Abednego (Daniel 3). Talk about a trial by fire—just like what you are going through. They "would not bow down to the idol" but trusted God to deliver them. But if not, they were still going to serve God. Of course we know that God DID deliver them and mightily. They came through the trial unharmed and knowing God as never before—not a hair on their heads harmed. (This is what I have prayed for you and your children.) They did not even have the smell of smoke on them. But here's the lesser-seen part: *They went into the fire bound—in the process they became loosed!* (Daniel 3:24–25). All they lost was their bondage.

I am praying that you will see God move on your behalf as wonderfully and mightily as these three did and that you will see the truths God has already given you to be true in your experience. Finally, I believe that you have never been more God's precious and chosen vessel than now. Imagine how he will be able to use your victory in the lives of others.

Love in Christ,
Kim

I notice a few things about this e-mail. First, she was reading God's Word. In essence, speaking truth to herself. Next, she spoke the truth to her friend, who confirmed it, and as she points out so well, that served as an "exclamation point." I don't think either of these women will forget the truths they discovered and discussed. Finally, she recounted the truths to me, using her own words *and* applying it to my situation. And to think she did all that without reading today's lesson. Pretty cool, huh?

Let's follow Kim's lead. Let's "pay attention and listen to the sayings of the wise." Let's apply our hearts to what God's Word teaches, for it is pleasing when we keep them in our hearts and have all of them ready on our lips . . . and our e-mail fingertips!

Stand at the Crossroads and Look:

1. Think of a new truth you've learned in the last week (it could be from this book or another source). Now think of a person you can speak that truth to and consider how the truth applies to her situation. Describe.

2. Take a few moments to write a note or to call that person today.

3. Can you think of a time when someone "spoke truth" to you in a way that was truly life changing? Who? What were the truths s/he shared?

4. Write out a prayer asking God to show you a new truth that you can share with others this coming week.

5. What key lesson did you glean from today's study?

Truths to Stand Upon:

- Sharing a truth with someone forces you to process and synthesize the information in such a way that it actually goes into a deeper part of your brain.
- When you go beyond sharing what you've learned to actually *applying* it to a specific situation, it is even more firmly planted in your mind.

Day Four

The Power of Confirmation

But to the Reubenites, the Gadites and the half-tribe of Manasseh, Joshua said, "Remember the command that Moses the servant of the Lord gave you: 'The Lord your God is giving you rest and has granted you this land.' Your wives, your children and your livestock may stay in the land that Moses gave you east of the Jordan, but all your fighting men, fully armed, must cross over ahead of your brothers. You are to help your brothers until the Lord gives them rest, as he has done for you, and until they too have taken possession of the land that the Lord your God is giving them. After that, you may go back and occupy your own land, which Moses the servant of the Lord gave you east of the Jordan toward the sunrise."

Then they answered Joshua, "Whatever you have commanded us we will do, and wherever you send us we will go. Just as we fully obeyed Moses, so we will obey you. Only may the Lord your God be with you as he was with Moses. Whoever rebels against your word and does not obey your words, whatever you may command them, will be put to death. Only be strong and courageous!"

Joshua 1:12–18

I notice several remarkable things about this passage. For example, I have studied the book of Joshua over and over, and I find no evidence that Joshua's friends were on hand when God spoke to him in chapter one, commanding him to be "strong and courageous." Yet here they use those exact same words! Isn't that incredible? When we speak truth to one another, we invariably confirm what God has already been speaking to our hearts.

Even as I have written this book, I have been so encouraged as God has used his people to send confirmation. Don't rob your brothers and sisters of a blessing. Speak the truth into their lives and be a source of confirmation!

The second thing I notice is that now that they (the various "ites" mentioned) have found rest; God wants them to help their brothers "until the Lord gives them rest" and "until they too have taken possession of the land." It's not enough for us to discover and rest in God's truth. We have to help our brothers, and especially our sisters, find that rest and "take possession" of all that God has for them. We need to help one another grab hold of the truth. I am so thankful for the people who have allowed God to use them in my life in such a way.

I mentioned last week my encounter with Hope Flinchbaugh. Here is her assessment of what happened that night; here is the truth she felt God was revealing. Although her letter is to me personally, the truths apply to all of us, so I want to speak those truths into your life as well.

Dear Donna,

I can't get this analogy out of my mind. I've seen this since the first time you told me that Beaver College is where it all started. Please listen to David's story, *your* story here:

David was sent to the battle line, not to fight giants, but to deliver cheese and bread and find out the welfare of his brothers. You accepted the same assignment, showing up at the conference to deliver "cheese and bread" to those who wanted your teachings, and to glean what God would have you to glean from the conference.

Like David, you did not run and hide from your Goliath. David faced his Goliath. In choosing to go to the Philadelphia conference, you faced your Goliath, too, Donna. Furthermore, David *ran toward* his giant, declaring the power and might of God all the way. In receiving prayer so willingly that night, you, too, faced the giant and ran toward him, hurling your stones and slinging until that giant fell down dead. He was conquered.

Interestingly, all the "smaller enemy" immediately ran as they were chased by the Israelites and scattered. Although the Philistines were scared that day, they later continued to be a staunch enemy of Israel. You've experienced the same victory. The giant is slain, the enemy ran in fear, but they're planning a comeback.

The same victory is yours today and tomorrow that was yours that day at the college. David knew the heart of God and loved Him above all else. He was *confident* that God would save him from every enemy.

Donna, I keep sensing that it may help you tremendously to look over that portion of David's life and the next five or ten years that followed. I believe God will use his Word to point out to you where you are now and where he's taking you. You have God's love, God's favor, strong upon you. Be confident in that. He has little wars here and there that he wants you to fight. One day you'll find yourself leading other people through the same victory that you've embraced, and like David, you'll be as a king among many who are longing for godly leadership.

Peace and grace to you as you continue to seek him. When God set me free from all the abuse, I prayed, "Lord, let me take some prisoners out with me." I knew there were others who desperately longed to be free from the torment and fear, and harbor safely in the arms of God.

Much love in Christ Jesus,
Hope Flinchbaugh

What a letter, huh? May I be bold? When is the last time YOU wrote a letter like that? When is the last time you spoke powerful truth into the life of another person? My guess is, it's been a long time. And so I would challenge you: Sit down with a pen and paper or get behind your computer screen. Then pray, asking God to give you some life-changing truths to share with a sister who is in desperate need of rest. Having been set free ourselves, it is only right that we should want to take a few prisoners out with us.

Stand at the Crossroads and Look:

1. Note your reaction to Hope's letter.

2. You have an assignment today! Pray and ask God to empower you, to show you the truths he wants you to share with someone. Write a letter that the recipient would consider worth saving and worth sharing with others. It's a tall order, but God's Word is filled with powerful truths. Choose one, then personalize and apply it.

3. Write out a prayer, asking God to continually show you truths worth sharing with others.

4. What key lesson did you glean from today's study?

Truths to Stand Upon:

- Having been set free ourselves, it is only right that we should want to take a few prisoners out with us.
- It's not enough for us to discover and rest in God's truth. We must help our sisters find rest and "take possession" of all that God has for them.

Day Five

No Condemnation

Therefore, there is now no condemnation for those who are in Christ Jesus.

Romans 8:1

I've gotten into a bad habit lately. I've started talking to people on airplanes. Conversation between total strangers in such circumstances seems quite unnecessary to me. I'd much rather read or sleep. Especially since I'm not one of those Christians who manages to lead everyone who sits in the window seat to Christ. To the contrary, I'm one of those Christians who manages to annoy the person in the aisle seat. Since I've never observed anything particularly redemptive emerge from my midair conversations, I've learned to keep my mouth shut. Most of my row-mates seem thrilled with my decision.

Like I said, though, lately I've been breaking my "buckle your mouth when you buckle your seat belt" policy, designed to prevent my fellow passengers from bolting for the nearest emergency exit. Last week, I got trapped in the dreaded middle seat. As I sat pondering what unpardonable sin in my life could have landed me in such virtual purgatory, I noted the body language of the woman in the window seat. It screamed, "Please don't talk to me or I'll jump."

Never one to pay the least attention to such relational cues, I launched into nonstop dialogue anyway. She disagreed with every word I uttered and frequently seemed offended, but that didn't slow me down. Unfortunately, I was in baggage claim by the time I realized she was offended. These profound little insights never come to me until long *after* the conversation. That's progress, though. The old Donna never had any relational insights *ever*. Now I get them after the fact. Some day, I may get them right in the midst of the interaction, like normal human beings do!

Okay, so back to the airplane. I can't remember her name and I hope she doesn't remember mine, because now that I think about it, I'm convinced she didn't particularly like me. And I can't remember what topic we were discussing, but it had something to do with human conflict throughout the panorama of human history. (I always keep the conversation light!)

But I do remember her explanation for the problem at hand. She called it "emotional cannibalism." Cannibals eat their enemies, not because they like the taste, but because they think the very act of consuming another human being will make them more powerful. Emotional cannibalism is the belief that we become more powerful by consuming other people. That somehow, we can build ourselves up by putting others down. We'd do well to remember that "it doesn't make one person more holy to point out the sin of another."[7]

An alarming number of Christians seem to take an almost fiendish delight in the demise of others. Rather than speaking truth, they enjoy speaking words of criticism and condemnation. I've made a careful study of the four Gospel records, and here's what I have concluded:

> The only people Jesus ever condemned were those who condemned others.

The only people he didn't want to spend time with were people who spent their time in self-congratulation. The ultimate sin is trying to ascend to God's place as judge and jury over the universe. Lately, I've taken to playing my own version of "Who Wants to Be a Millionaire?" at my speaking engagements. Instead, we play "Who Wants to Be a PWA?"[8] and the reward is something better than a million dollars. The winner receives her very own, not-available-in-stores PWA T-shirt. The game has only one question. See if you can get it right. Go ahead and poll the audience or call upon your lifeline if you have to. Here comes the big question:

WHY WAS SATAN KICKED OUT OF HEAVEN?

a. He had sex outside of marriage

---

[7] Amy Grant interview with CCM magazine.
[8] PWA stands for Princess with Attitude. This is my most popular teaching, found in my book *Walking in Total God-Confidence*.

b. He went through a really messy divorce

c. He got a tattoo and pierced his tongue

d. The sin of pride

The correct answer (imagine music playing) is: d. The sin of pride.

Okay, we had our fun. But this is serious stuff, my friends. When you condemn others, you are immediately condemning yourself, because you are not God yet you are putting yourself in the place of God. That's the sin of pride, and God hates it, big time.

In speaking to the woman caught in the act of adultery, Jesus said, "Neither do I condemn you. . . . Go now and leave your life of sin" (John 8:11). He didn't say, "You piece of trash. You're gonna fry." He extended mercy. He also extended mercy to a woman who'd been divorced *five times* (John 4:7–30). Notice he didn't get into an elaborate discussion about whether or not she had "grounds" for any of those divorces. If either of these women walked into the average church today, they'd serve her for breakfast!

I don't think there is any more important truth we can speak into the lives of our fellow man than today's Scripture: "There is now no condemnation for those who are in Christ Jesus." As a wise friend recently pointed out to me, "The truth is, we are all just three choices and half an hour from catastrophe."[9] Think about it:

1. You hop in your car and drive to a certain street corner.
2. You buy heroin.
3. You inject it into your veins.

Three choices. Half an hour. Your life is ruined. It could happen to someone you love. Sounds incredible? A minister to street people spoke at a Sunday school class I attended not long ago. He shared the stories of several prostitutes he was working with. One of the women had been a surgical nurse; her husband was a prominent doctor. One day, she chose to take a pill to stay awake during the night shift. She became addicted. She began stealing the pills. She got fired from her job. Her husband divorced her. She ended up living on the streets. She became a hooker. Boom. Boom. Boom.

---

[9]My thanks to the inimitable Jason Easton for this clever little ditty.

In my previous book, I shared how my best friend's son made a series of choices that ruined his life. He chose to take drugs. He chose to buy a gun. He chose to shoot a police officer. Three choices. Boom. Boom. Boom. Now this godly woman, a homeschooling mother of four children, must routinely travel to federal prison to visit her son.

The next time you see someone you are tempted to condemn, remember that nurse. Remember my friend's son. There's a world filled with hurting people who need to know the truth: Jesus Christ came to pay the price for their foolish choices.

Will you condemn them? Or will you speak the truth to them? You can't do both.

Stand at the Crossroads and Look:

1. What is emotional cannibalism?

2. Have you been guilty of practicing it?

3. Is there someone you have condemned . . . rather than extended mercy to? How can you reach out to that person?

4. Write out a prayer asking God to give you a heart of compassion rather than condemnation.

5. What key lesson did you glean from today's study?

6. Write out This Week's Verse from memory.

Truths to Stand Upon:

- The only people Jesus condemned were those who condemned others.
- There's a world filled with hurting people. Will you condemn them? Or will you speak the truth to them?

Weekly Review

Take a few moments to fill in the ten actions and attitudes required to Stand Firm. Look in the back of the book if you need help.

S _____ God first

S _____ God's perspective

S _____ your spiritual hunger

S _____ the love God has for you

S _____ yourself against the attacks of the enemy

S _____ truth to yourself and others

S _____ the tide of mediocrity

S _____ like a saint

S _____ wholeheartedly

S _____ firm until the end

WEEK SEVEN:
Stem the Tide of Mediocrity

This Week's Verse:

Jesus answered, "I am the way and the truth and the life. No
one comes to the Father except through me."

John 14:6

Day One

Plastic Answers for Real Problems

Jesus answered, "I am the way and the truth and the life. No one comes to the Father except through me."

John 14:6

I have a complete collection of Christian marriage books. In fact, if I were to cash them in for the original retail price, I could probably pay off Haiti's National Debt. Some had helpful ideas, but none ever got to the root of the problem. None ever dared go within a mile of the truth.

My personal all-time favorite marriage book is the one now famous for advocating Saran Wrap as a solution to marital disharmony. Hey, you've got a problem? No problem! Wrap yourself in a little Saran Wrap and *Voila!* No more problems!!! (This is the point in the speech where I wave my Cinderella light-up, musical magic wand. Ask me to show it to you sometime. I will wave it over your head, and all *your* problems will be solved instantly.)

Well, guess what? I tried the blue Saran Wrap and the pink Saran Wrap and the clear Saran Wrap. And I still had marriage problems by the truckload. I think we should pass a law that people with great marriages aren't allowed to write marriage books. They just haven't got a CLUE what they are talking about! All they do is make the rest of us feel bad.

But it's not just marriage books that offer plastic answers for real problems. Another time, I read a "generic" how-to-be-a-good-Christian book in which the author, a pastor, stated that he could tell the spiritual condition of any member of his congregation simply by looking at her car. *Oh, no. I'm finished.* I thought to myself. *My car is literally a trash can on wheels.*[1]

Then one day, I was pulling my *trash can on wheels* out of my garage. And since I was late, as usual (and it wasn't 'cause I spent extra time in prayer and meditation, either!), I was flying out of the garage. And I crashed into a tree. There went the taillight. I did some checking and found out it would cost almost $300 to fix it. Since I don't have an extra $300 floating around, I didn't do anything about it.

Then one day, speeding along the freeway, minding my own business, I heard a rather ominous sound coming up behind me. Yep. It was a policeman. He pointed out that I had a problem.

I cried.

It worked.

Sometimes it pays to be a woman. Anyway, when I explained to the nice officer that I simply didn't have enough money to get it fixed properly, he said, "No problem. Just get some red SARAN WRAP and tape it over the light." Problem solved. (We need another wave of the Cinderella magic wand here, don't ya think?)

Hey, I guess it turns out that plastic answers really DO solve real-world problems after all. So I've decided to entitle my next book, *The Miracle Healing Powers of Saran Wrap.* Who wants to place the first order? Remember, if you call now, you'll also get the ginsu knives and the Tupperware. But hurry. Orders will not last! Dial 1-800-Saran-Wrap.

I'll be waiting for your call.

Seriously, if we want to touch our world in a significant way, it's time to leave the Saran Wrap in the kitchen where it belongs. If we are ever to stem the time of mediocrity in the church, it's got to start with putting away plastic answers and offering real solutions for real people in the real world.

People don't need Saran Wrap. They need Jesus, who said, "I am the way and the truth and the life" (John 14:6). We can't offer them

---

[1]A note for the detail-oriented (like my dear sweet editor), who are sitting there thinking, "Didn't she tell us that she got a new car?" Yep, I did. This story is about my old car. But to tell you the truth, I've already done a remarkable job of turning my new car into a trash can on wheels!

both. We can only offer one or the other. Will we offer the Real Answer or a cheap substitute?

Stand at the Crossroads and Look:

1. Can you think of a time in your life when you were offered a "Saran Wrap" solution for a real problem? How did that make you feel? What were the results?

2. Have you ever been guilty of offering someone else "Saran Wrap" solutions? What was the result?

3. Ask God to show you if you need to go to that person again, this time demonstrating a compassionate understanding.

4. Write out a prayer asking God to show you any areas of your life where you've fallen into "Saran Wrap" thinking. Express your desire to be a channel of real answers to a hurting world.

5. What key lesson did you glean from today's study?

Truths to Stand Upon:

- If we want to touch our world in a significant way, it's time to leave the Saran Wrap in the kitchen where it belongs.
- We must offer real solutions for real people in the real world.

Day Two

Bait and Switch

Brothers, think of what you were when you were called. Not many of you were wise by human standards; not many were influential; not many were of noble birth. But God chose the foolish things of the world to shame the wise; God chose the weak things of the world to shame the strong. He chose the lowly things of this world and the despised things—and the things that are not—to nullify the things that are, so that no one may boast before him.

1 Corinthians 1:26–29

Just when you thought you could somehow make sense out of my weird life, here's a zinger for ya: I attended Wharton, arguably the most prestigious business school in the world. Of course, I only managed to take a few classes before I "remembered" that nothing good was supposed to happen in my life and (deliberately but subconsciously) let the whole thing fall to pieces. I honestly feel sorry for those of you who know what I'm talking about.

Anyway, one of the classes I took was Marketing 101. And the lesson most vividly emblazoned in my mind concerned "Bait and Switch." Bait and Switch is a little technique frequently used by retail stores. Here's how it works: They advertise a fabulous deal on a top-quality item they know people won't be able to resist. That's the Bait. When customers come flocking into the store, hoping for the deal of the century, the store just "happens" to be sold out. So they are offered a cheap replacement. Nine times out of ten, people will settle for it because they'd rather go home with something than nothing. That's the Switch.

Now this is important, folks: Retail stores only pull the Bait and Switch routine when they think the "real deal" they can offer you isn't good enough. If what they had to offer was good enough, they'd just advertise it and be done with it.

I think a lot of Christians are pulling the old Bait and Switch routine on the world. Churches do it, parachurch organizations do it, and individual Christians do it. It's a mind set that says, "Anything to get them into the Kingdom." We promise health, wealth, and a professional football career. In my more cynical moments, I've observed that everyone in a sporting event, a beauty contest, prison, or rehab is a born-again Christian. Why? Because they are prime candidates to fall for the Bait and Switch. They are in pressure situations that set them up for easy believism. For the record, I've competed in both beauty contests *and* sporting events; I've been arrested more than once and am a recovering drug addict who is currently working a twelve-step program. So I'm not casting aspersions here. Just sharing some observations I've made along the journey.

I remember a time when I was considering volunteering with an organization that ministered to high school students. I was good friends with a staff member and had attended some of their events with her. Then, one night, she invited me to a planning meeting. They sang and prayed. They talked about past successes and future plans with great enthusiasm. It all sounded so wonderful; I was ready to get on board. Then one of the staff said she had a serious problem they needed to discuss.

Here's the serious problem: An unpopular student from a poor family had asked to host an upcoming event at his home. The room began to buzz. They were at a loss to know what to do. It was *obvious* to everyone in the room that they couldn't let him host an event. I specifically remember one senior staff member emphasizing to the rest, with gravity in his voice, that ALL of their events had to be hosted by football players and cheerleaders or other "student leaders." They had to be sure they were located at beautiful homes belonging to popular kids . . . or no one would come.

At first, I thought they were joking. Or testing me.

Actually, they were serious, and they were completely ignoring me, because they were so engrossed in this great struggle on behalf of the Kingdom of God.

I felt sick to my stomach. And I wondered how these kids were gonna feel when they got into the real world, in the real church. I wondered how bitter and disillusioned they were going to become when they didn't get what they signed up for. I wondered how they were gonna feel when they realized they fell for the old Bait and Switch.

I mean, have you looked around the pews lately? Most churches aren't exactly filled with the rich and famous or the bold and the beautiful. First Corinthians 1:26–29 reminds us:

> Brothers, think of what you were when you were called. Not many of you were wise by human standards; not many were influential; not many were of noble birth. But God chose the foolish things of the world to shame the wise; God chose the weak things of the world to shame the strong. He chose the lowly things of this world and the despised things—and the things that are not—to nullify the things that are, so that no one may boast before him.

I may offend some people here, but I've got to tell you: I have a real problem with organizations that insist on holding up "beautiful people" and "heroes" (whether sports or business) as if they were typical of life in the Kingdom. It ain't so. Most of the Christians I know are just like me: ordinary people living ordinary lives in humble service to an extraordinary God.

The reality of the Christian walk isn't flashy, isn't sexy, and it doesn't sell cars. We can't offer people the world on a silver platter, but we can offer them a personal relationship with the living God. Remember: the Bait and Switch is only useful when you think what you've *really* got to offer isn't good enough. Let's stop baiting people. Let's tell them the plain truth of the Gospel of Jesus Christ. It's been more than sufficient to bring people into the Kingdom for nearly 2,000 years. There's no need to switch it now.

Stand at the Crossroads and Look:

1. Have you ever seen the Bait and Switch in action? Describe.

2. Have you ever been guilty of pulling the Bait and Switch on someone?

3. Write out a prayer of repentance to God, confessing the truth that the *real* gospel is more than sufficient to advance the Kingdom.

4. What key lesson did you glean from today's study?

Truths to Stand Upon:

- The Bait and Switch is only used when you don't think what you've really got to offer is good enough.
- The real Gospel has been bringing people into the Kingdom for 2,000 years; there's no need to switch now.

Day Three

Rich and Poor

Do you not know that in a race all the runners run, but only one gets the prize? Run in such a way as to get the prize. Everyone who competes in the games goes into strict training. They do it to get a crown that will not last; but we do it to get a crown that will last forever. Therefore I do not run like a man running aimlessly; I do not fight like a man beating the air. No, I beat my body and make it my slave so that after I have preached to others, I myself will not be disqualified for the prize.

1 Corinthians 9:24–27

Have I been advocating mediocrity in the section on stemming the tide of mediocrity?

That's the thought that flashed through my mind during a break, when I went downstairs to have a cup of coffee and catch some of the 2000 Summer Olympics. I mean, so far I've said I don't trust people with perfect marriages and am suspicious of anyone who is beautiful or famous. Am I saying that failure is inherently more spiritual than success? (I'm thinking out loud here. . . .)

The church is a fascinating bundle of contradictions. When I was a brand-new believer, I attended a church that equated success with God's blessing. So the most respected members of the congregation were the wealthy. We figured God must *really* love and esteem them since he rewarded them with success and entrusted them with so many resources. If you drove a Mercedes, everyone looked up to you. These Christians had biblical precedent on their side: Throughout the Old Testament, God's blessings were manifested in material wealth. All the patriarchs were filthy rich, weren't they? If Solomon were alive today, he would not only be a millionaire, but a *billionaire*.

Then I went off to college and began attending a church filled with equally sincere Christians who believed the polar opposite. In this church, we esteemed people who lived in the poorest neighborhoods of the city in run-down apartment buildings and drove beat-up old Honda Civics. We were inherently suspicious of successful businessmen and anyone else with money. Obviously, they had their priorities all wrong. I mean, didn't Jesus say, "Sell all you have and give to the poor"? Didn't Jesus largely ignore the wealthy Pharisees and minister instead to the downtrodden?

Over the past three years, I've had the privilege of ministering at churches all over the country. Some filled with very poor people. Some liberally sprinkled with very rich people. A handful had a beautiful mixture of rich and poor, although such churches are an exception rather than the rule. Guess what I discovered? There are wonderful Christians in poor churches; people who are clearly in the center of God's will for their lives. Christians who are obviously living well above the level of mediocrity. And there are equally wonderful Christians in rich churches; people who are clearly in the center of God's will for their lives. Christians who are obviously living well above the level of mediocrity.

Mediocrity has nothing to do with being rich or poor. There are mediocre rich people and mediocre poor people. There are successful people who are spiritually mediocre, and there are people who are absolute failures, by the world's standards, who are spiritual giants.

It's not *where* you live, but *how* you live that matters. And we're all called to live with determination and zeal:

> Do you not know that in a race all the runners run, but only one gets the prize? Run in such a way as to get the prize. Everyone who competes in the games goes into strict training. They do it to get a crown that will not last; but we do it to get a crown that will last forever. Therefore I do not run like a man running aimlessly; I do not fight like a man beating the air. No, I beat my body and make it my slave so that after I have preached to others, I myself will not be disqualified for the prize. (1 Corinthians 9:24–27)

Since God's heart is for *all* people, it makes sense that he would place *his* people at every station of life. Think about it, a marathon runner wouldn't do the U.S. Olympic team much good competing in the 100-meter sprint. Our fastest swimmer wouldn't do the gymnastics team a bit of good. Just like the U.S. Olympic team needs different athletes to compete in the various races, so God needs Christians in various social circles. He requires each of us to be faithful to give everything we've got to the race set before us. The point is simply this: Whatever race God has called you to run, run to win.

Stand at the Crossroads and Look:

1. Who are you inclined to think are more spiritual: rich or poor people?

2. Did today's lesson change your point of view at all? Why or why not?

3. Do you think it's possible to be "successful" and spiritually mediocre? How about a "failure" and a spiritual giant? Why?

4. What race has God called you to run? Are you running it with all you've got?

5. Write out a prayer asking God to help you stem the tide of mediocrity in whatever social circle he has placed you.

6. What key lesson did you glean from today's study?

Truths to Stand Upon:

- Mediocrity has nothing to do with being rich or poor. It's not *where* you live, but *how* you live that matters.
- Whatever race God has called you to run, run to win.

Day Four

The Number of Our Days

*Teach us to number our days aright,
  that we may gain a heart of wisdom.*   Psalm 90:12

Brace yourself. I have one more story to tell about my chickens. I promise this will be the last. Okay, let's go back to that fateful day when I came home and discovered that Dinker (aka Dumber) had virtually wiped out the entire flock. And let's look at the events that led up to this heart-wrenching moment.

Early in the morning, my four-year-old Tara had gone out to visit the goats and chickens on her own. Now this is something Tara knows she is not allowed to do. And frankly, even though I *knew* she had snuck out of the house and strongly suspected where she had gone, I did nothing about it. Why? Because it was easier to look the other way than to deal with her disobedience. I had more important things to do with my time.

Among the many reasons why Tara isn't supposed to visit the goat pen unsupervised is that she isn't capable of closing the gate properly. Sure enough, shortly after Tara returned to the house, I looked out the window and saw that the goats were on the loose.

I told Leah, my ten year old, to put the goats away. She ignored me. I waited five minutes and told her again. She ignored me. I waited ten minutes and told her *again*, but this time I was clearly aggravated: *Put those goats away NOW*, I commanded forcefully. She ignored me anyway.

I knew she was ignoring me. But I didn't do anything about it. Because somehow, in my warped little brain, it seemed easier to look the other way than to deal with her disobedience. I was thinking strictly short-term. I was thinking, "I don't have time to stop what I'm doing." I was thinking I could somehow *save time*.

Okay, so I wasn't thinking.

So I've got two kids in flat-out disobedience and two goats wandering the property. But hey, I'm *saving time*, right?

Later in the day, we were rushing out the door to run some errands. I noticed that the goats were *still* out, and I was furious. I yelled at the children, but I didn't do anything about it. I didn't have time; I was in a hurry.

While we were gone, the chickens wandered through the gate and out into the open, which proved to be more temptation than Dinker could handle. The rest of the tale has already been told. Except the part about the funerals.

Having saved five minutes by not bringing Tara in from the goat pen,

Having saved five minutes by not walking Leah *out* to the goat pen to make sure she put them away,

Having saved five minutes by rushing off to run errands rather than refusing to leave until Leah put the goats away,

I spent three hours digging graves, in the pitch dark, in solid granite earth. Since I couldn't dig very deep, the dogs kept digging up the dead chickens which had to be reburied so many times I lost count. Each funeral was more gruesome than the one before. Besides all this earth-moving activity, I spent countless additional hours, over the course of several weeks, comforting my crying children. I saved a few minutes and wasted dozens of hours.

Minute wise. Hour foolish.

That's me.

Is it you, too? Are you minute wise and hour foolish?

We don't invest a few minutes each day in Scripture memory, so we waste hours (weeks? months? years?) wrestling with decisions that should be no-brainers. We don't invest a few minutes each day reading the Word of God, so we waste years of our lives in disobedience and fruitless folly. We don't invest sixty to ninety minutes attending church faithfully, so we live in spiritual weakness for the rest of the week. We don't invest a few minutes each day with a prayer partner, so we lead unaccountable lives that cost us hours of personal anguish.

We're minute wise and hour foolish.

For some reason, I find great comfort knowing I'm not the only one squandering time. During a lifetime, the average American[2] spends:

6 months at traffic lights
1 year searching for misplaced objects (for me, it will be more like ten years because I *save time* by not bothering to put things back where they belong)
8 months opening junk mail
2 years calling phone numbers that are busy/people who are not available
3 years in meetings
5 years waiting in lines
10+ years watching television

I'm not sure any of those activities qualify as minute wise, but they are certainly hour foolish.

How do you spend your time? Let me challenge you to do something this next week: Take a Time Inventory. Here's how it works: Photocopy or recreate the Time Inventory Chart that follows. The prep work involves listing thirty of your most-frequent activities. I've listed ten to get you started. Once your numbering system is worked out, you can simply write the appropriate number in the corresponding time slot. It's easier to plug in numbers than to write out the activities each time. (That's minute wise *and* hour wise!)

Then, for one week, carry the chart with you wherever you go and jot down how you spend the better part of each half hour. TV. Housework. Reading. Praying. Daydreaming. And don't suddenly spend two hours in prayer so you won't look minute wise and hour foolish on paper. Be honest and try to follow your normal routine as much as possible. I first did this exercise in 1982. If you're anything like me, this little wake-up call may be a turning point in your life.

If we would stem the tide of mediocrity, we must start thinking about how we spend our minutes. If we do, the hours will take care of themselves. Let's ask God to "teach us to number our days aright, that we may gain a heart of wisdom." Then, when we reflect upon our lifetime, we'll be able to say we lived:

Minute wise. Hour wiser.

---

[2]Notes taken from a Greg Laurie sermon I once heard.

Stand at the Crossroads and Look:

1. In what ways are you minute wise, hour foolish?

2. Prepare to conduct a Time Inventory for the next seven days.

3. Write out a prayer asking God to teach you to number your days aright, that you might gain a heart of wisdom.

4. What key lesson did you glean from today's study?

Truths to Stand Upon:

- Beware the temptation to live minute wise and hour foolish.
- If we would stem the tide of mediocrity, we must use our minutes wisely.

Time Inventory Chart

Time	Mon	Tues	Wed	Thur	Fri	Sat	Sun	Activity
6:00								1. Praying
6:30								2. Bible
7:00								Reading
7:30								3. Fellowship
8:00								4. Service
8:30								5. TV
9:00								6. Phone
9:30								7. Grooming
10:00								8. Meals
10:30								9. Dishes
11:00								10. Sleeping
11:30								11.
Noon								12.
12:30								13.
1:00								14.
1:30								15.
2:00								16.
2:30								17.
3:00								18.
3:30								19.
4:00								20.
4:30								21.
5:00								22.
5:30								23.
6:00								24.
6:30								25.
7:00								26.
7:30								27.
8:00								28.
8:30								29.
9:00								30.
9:30								
10:00								
10:30								
11:00								

Adapted with permission from Michael LeBoeuf, *Working Smart.*

Day Five

Spur One Another On

Let us hold unswervingly to the hope we profess, for he who promised is faithful. And let us consider how we may spur one another on toward love and good deeds. Let us not give up meeting together, as some are in the habit of doing, but let us encourage one another—and all the more as you see the Day approaching.

Hebrews 10:23–25

Every morning at 7:00 A.M. my phone rings. It's my prayer partner, Deb Lovett, calling me from Ohio. We rarely talk. We pray. And then we hang up. If we want to update our prayer list, we e-mail each other. Well, I got an e-mail from Deb on a certain Monday, telling me she wouldn't be able to call on Thursday because she was going to the zoo with her son's class.

FANTASTIC! I thought. I can sleep in!!! Oh, how I relished the thought. An extra hour of sleep? Wouldn't that just be heavenly? Wouldn't an extra hour of sleep just set me up for life? All day Monday, all day Tuesday, all day Wednesday, I looked forward to those extra minutes under the covers. That's why I was stunned on Thursday morning when at 7:03 A.M. the phone rang. The woman on the other end said, "Hi, this is so-and-so calling from Virginia."

I roared with laughter.

The woman thought I was nuts. She didn't know anything about me, my Ohio prayer partner, or the extra hour of sleep she had just cost me. I tried to explain. "Listen, I don't know why you *think* you called me this morning. But trust me, you called so we could pray." We chatted for a while, then prayed together.

Her call was just the "spur" I needed that morning to get up and get going.

You know what a spur is, right? During my routine visits to the feed store, I get an eyefull of spurs. There's a whole wall full of 'em. (If you think I'm making this up, come visit me and I'll show you!) If you're not fortunate enough to live in a cowboy town like I do, maybe you need a bit of enlightenment. A spur is a round metal device which attaches to the back of a cowboy boot. The rider lightly kicks, or spurs, the horse to get him moving in the right direction.

A spur should hurt, but just a little. It should be just enough to make you uncomfortable with standing around doin' nothin'. Just enough to get you moving. You don't want someone spurring you so hard that she *draws blood*, if you catch my drift.

So let me ask you: Who spurs *you* on? Who kicks you out of bed and gets you praying first thing in the morning? Maybe you're one of those spiritual giants who doesn't need a spur. Praise God and may your tribe increase. But for the rest of us mere mortals, we need a spur.

I guess this is my week to set forth challenges, because I want to set forth another one: I want you to invite someone to be your spur. Specifically, I want you to track down someone who will call you every day, thirty minutes before you normally wake up. Conversely, you can find someone who will let you call *her* thirty minutes before you normally wake up. (Get it: if you have to call her, *you* have to wake up.) Remember, this is not phone time. This is *prayer time*. So pray and hang up.

Once you have finished praying, devote the remainder of that half hour to reading and studying God's Word. Eventually, you'll enjoy this ritual so much, you'll ask your spur to call you an *hour* before you normally wake up.

Of course, one spur isn't enough for some of us. I need lots of spurs in my life. Kathleen McQuain, my weekly women's Bible study teacher, spurs me on in Scripture memory. Each term we study a Christian book together, so I always have material to read and ponder. And there's always plenty of homework to do. Marita Littauer has spurred me on in my latest endeavor to read through the Bible in a year, using *The Narrated Bible*. My kids have been doing an awesome job of spurring me on in my new fitness program. (They have told me in no uncertain terms that they *don't* want an ever-expanding mommy!) You, my readers, spur me on to learn new truths to share.

Who spurs you on?

Who are you spurring?

If we would stem the tide of mediocrity in our midst, then we must be committed to actively "spur one another on toward love and good deeds." And we must be willing to let others "spur" us, even when it's slightly painful, even when it's inconvenient, even when we'd rather sleep in.

Stand at the Crossroads and Look:

1. In what areas of your life do you need a spur? Morning prayer/ devotions? Bible reading? Weekly Bible study? Scripture memory? Using your gifts? Others?

2. Who can you ask to spur you on in each of these areas? (Select a different spur for each area of need.)

3. Make a list of people who might be willing to call you thirty minutes before you normally wake up.

4. Okay, start calling. And keep calling until you find someone who is willing to spur you on.

5. Write out a prayer asking God to show you the people you need to invite into your life to spur you on.

6. What key lesson did you glean from today's study?

7. Write out This Week's Verse from memory.

Truths to Stand Upon:

- To stem the tide of mediocrity, be committed to actively "spur one another on toward love and good deeds."
- Invite others to spur you on in your spiritual growth.

Weekly Review:

Take a few moments to fill in the ten actions and attitudes required to Stand Firm. Look in the back of the book if you need help.

S _____ God first

S _____ God's perspective

S _____ your spiritual hunger

S _____ the love God has for you

S _____ yourself against the attacks of the enemy

S _____ truth to yourself and others

S _____ the tide of mediocrity

S _____ like a saint

S _____ wholeheartedly

S _____ firm until the end

WEEK EIGHT:
Suffer Like a Saint

This Week's Verse:

Though the fig tree does not bud and there are no grapes on the vines, though the olive crop fails and the fields produce no food, though there are no sheep in the pen and no cattle in the stalls, yet I will rejoice in the Lord, I will be joyful in God my Savior.

Habakkuk 3:17–18

Day One

Suffering in a Fallen World

Though the fig tree does not bud
and there are no grapes on the vines,
though the olive crop fails
and the fields produce no food,
though there are no sheep in the pen
and no cattle in the stalls,
yet I will rejoice in the Lord,
I will be joyful in God my Savior.

Habakkuk 3:17–18

Sometimes crummy stuff happens. If you're like me, your first response is to look around for someone to *blame*. See, if I can blame someone, then the universe still makes sense. It's still a safe place to be, because you can just "deal" with the person who caused the trouble.

What scares me to death is when there's no one to blame. When forces are at work that are beyond human control. No logic. No apparent rhyme or reason. Nothing you could have done to prevent it; nothing you can do to stop it from happening again. Hurricanes. Earthquakes. Leukemia.

It's called living in a fallen world, and sometimes it just doesn't make sense. I call that Category #1 suffering. It's the kind of suffering that can overwhelm and incapacitate us, the kind that makes us question the goodness or power of God. Our finite minds look at it this way: Either God is good, but he wasn't powerful enough to prevent our suffering, or he had the power to prevent the suffering, but didn't bother to do so. Well, then, he must not be a very good God.

We struggle to make sense of a universe in which a God who is both all-powerful and all-loving lets famine strike, lets children starve to death by the thousands. We want to live in a world where one plus one always equals two; a place where IF you do this, THEN you get that. Sadly, that's not the real world.

Habakkuk was writing to people just like you and me. People who had done everything they knew how to do, but didn't get the results they were counting on. People for whom one plus one equaled zero.

These people had planted fig trees and tended grapevines, but they didn't grow *anyway*.

They farmed their land, but the crops failed *anyway*.

They had a place to put livestock, but they didn't have livestock *anyway*.

There's no indication that any of this was their *fault*; it just was. They were being buffeted by powerful forces beyond their control. The solution? Rejoice in the Lord *anyway*.

Why?

The verse goes on to tell us. It's because "The Sovereign Lord is my strength; he makes my feet like the feet of a deer, he enables me to go on the heights" (Habakkuk 3:19). Deer are surefooted creatures. They are able to stand firm, even on tough terrain.

Maybe you've done everything you know how to do to make your life work like it should, but have found yourself trapped in a storm *anyway*. God has promised to enable you to stand firm in the face of suffering. I think that's the essence of faith: *anyway*. It's no big deal to trust God when life is great. But to keep on trusting when life is downright awful, that's a whole different deal. Even as Job declared, "Though he slay me, yet will I trust in him" (Job 13:15, KJV). Anyway.

Do you have "anyway" kind of faith?

The apostle Paul did. I've written an entire book, *Becoming a Vessel God Can Use*, based on the following passage from 2 Corinthians 4:

> But we have this treasure in jars of clay to show that this all-surpassing power is from God and not from us. We are hard pressed on every side, but not crushed; perplexed, but not in despair; persecuted, but not abandoned; struck down, but not destroyed. We always carry around in our body the death of Jesus, so that the life of Jesus may also be revealed in our body. For we who are alive are always being given over to death for Jesus' sake, so that his life may be revealed in our mortal body. So then, death is at work in us, but life is at work in you.

It is written: "I believed; therefore I have spoken." With that same spirit of faith we also believe and therefore speak, because we know that the one who raised the Lord Jesus from the dead will also raise us with Jesus and present us with you in his presence. All this is for your benefit, so that the grace that is reaching more and more people may cause thanksgiving to overflow to the glory of God. (2 Corinthians 4:7–15)

That's "anyway" faith. I guess it's a matter of perspective. Do you view yourself as God's servant, willing to carry out whatever assignment he gives, willing to endure whatever hardship it requires? Or do you view God as *your* servant, who had better snap to it when you issue a command, I mean, um, offer up a prayer request? We are God's servants; he is not our servant.

We're back to Theology 101 here. Either we believe God loves us or we don't. Either we believe he is ruling the universe or we don't. If we believe God loves us and that he is in charge of what happens in the world, then we must receive EVERYTHING that comes our way as having first been filtered through the hands of a loving God. And we must be willing to stand firm and declare, as Jesus did, "Yet not as I will, but as you will" (Matthew 26:39).

Stand at the Crossroads and Look:

1. Have you experienced Category #1 suffering? The kind that *just happens*, and there's no one to blame?

2. How did that experience impact you? Did it cause you to doubt either the goodness or the power of God? Explain.

3. Do you tend to view yourself as a servant of God, or do you view God as your servant? Don't give the "correct" answer. Think about how you live your life and how you respond to suffering: That will give you the true answer.

4. Write out a prayer expressing your commitment to live as a servant of God in the midst of a fallen world.

5. What key lesson did you glean from today's study?

Truths to Stand Upon:

- We are God's servants; he is not our servant.
- If we believe God loves us and that he is in charge of what happens in the world, then we must receive EVERYTHING that comes our way as having first been filtered through the hands of a loving God.

Day Two

Suffering at the Hands of Fallen People

Whatever happens, conduct yourselves in a manner worthy of the gospel of Christ. Then, whether I come and see you or only hear about you in my absence, I will know that you stand firm in one spirit, contending as one man for the faith of the gospel without being frightened in any way by those who oppose you. This is a sign to them that they will be destroyed, but that you will be saved—and that by God. For it has been granted to you on behalf of Christ not only to believe on him, but also to suffer for him, since you are going through the same struggle you saw I had, and now hear that I still have.

Philippians 1:27–30

The second category of suffering is living among fallen people. Our fellow human beings hurt us in a myriad of ways, every day of our lives. They may hurt us physically, committing crimes against us like rape, incest, abuse, or assault. They can hurt us physically by "hitting us in the wallet." Bypassing us for the promotion we deserve. Overcharging us for products and services. They may hurt us emotionally through insults or abandonment.

Sometimes people intentionally set out to inflict pain upon us. More often, they hurt us because they have first been hurt. I often say, "hurt people hurt people" and "people in pain are a real pain."

If you examine the interpersonal dynamics in any home, office, church, or community, you'll invariably discover that those who cause the most turmoil are themselves in the most turmoil. If we can learn to deal with them *as a minister of the gospel*, perhaps we'd get a whole new perspective. Rather than focusing on how much the other person is hurting you, turn the tables and ask yourself: What is the source of her pain? How can I help alleviate that pain? How can I bring the mercy of Jesus to bear upon this situation? How can I be a channel of God's grace to this person?

As a wise woman once observed, "It's never about people." It helps me to remember, when I feel like a person is attacking me, to pause and consider, "Who is really launching this attack? Who is really behind it?" At the risk of sounding like someone who sees "a devil behind every rock," I'm increasingly convinced that the enemy, the evil one, is behind all human conflict.

I get bombarded with "forwards" over the Internet. (Please, please, please: Love me enough NOT to add me to your forward list.) I rarely read them, but some time ago, I got one that was not only worth reading, but it's also worth sharing. I think it will help us to prayerfully consider these words as we face the prospect of daily living among fallen people:

DO IT ANYWAY[1]

People are often unreasonable, illogical, and self-centered;
Forgive them, anyway.
If you are kind, people may accuse you of selfish, ulterior motives;
Be kind, anyway.
If you are successful, you will win some false friends and some
    true enemies;
Succeed, anyway.
If you are honest and frank, people may cheat you;
Be honest and frank, anyway.
What you spend years building, someone could destroy overnight;
Build, anyway.
If you find serenity and happiness, they may be jealous;
Be happy, anyway.
The good you do today, people will often forget tomorrow;
Do good, anyway.
Give the world the best you have, and it may never be enough;
Give the world the best you've got, anyway.
You see, in the final analysis, it is between you and God;
It was never between you and them, anyway.

There's that word again: Anyway.
That last sentence sums it up perfectly. It's not between you and

---

[1]Attributed to Mother Teresa.

them. It's between you and God. It's not about trusting people; it's about trusting God. It's about trusting that the God who rules the universe has, in his infinite wisdom, allowed this person to enter your world knowing full well how much pain she would inflict upon you. Rather than becoming angry with the person, ask God to show you the "why." Rather than becoming angry with God, *embrace* the why.

And when the "why" doesn't come—and let's be honest enough to admit: sometimes it never does—let's continue to trust God *anyway*. Whatever else may come of life's suffering, I always find great comfort in allowing God to redeem it. I often tell my children, "As Christians, we're in a win-win situation. If something wonderful happens, praise God. If something painful happens, it just opens more opportunities for us to serve God."

When you live among fallen people, you will suffer. Live joyfully among them *anyway*. Keep this thought always before you: "Whatever happens, conduct yourselves in a manner worthy of the gospel of Christ" (Philippians 1:27).

Stand at the Crossroads and Look:

1. Have you suffered at the hands of a fallen person? Describe.

2. Are you currently facing such a situation? Does it help to realize that "people in pain are a real pain"?

3. How can seeking to minister to the pain in that other person's heart help ease the pain s/he is causing you?

4. Respond to the poem, "Do It Anyway."

5. Write out a prayer asking God to show you the hurt that's motivating the person who is hurting/has hurt you the most. Ask him to show you how you might be an agent of grace to that person.

6. What key lesson did you glean from today's study?

Truths to Stand Upon:

- Hurt people hurt people. Rather than focusing on how someone has hurt you, consider how you might minister healing to *her*.
- When you live among fallen people, you will suffer. Live joyfully among them *anyway*.

Day Three

Suffering as a Fallen Person

I do not understand what I do. For what I want to do I do not do, but what I hate I do. And if I do what I do not want to do, I agree that the law is good. As it is, it is no longer I myself who do it, but it is sin living in me. I know that nothing good lives in me, that is, in my sinful nature. For I have the desire to do what is good, but I cannot carry it out. For what I do is not the good I want to do; no, the evil I do not want to do—this I keep on doing. Now if I do what I do not want to do, it is no longer I who do it, but it is sin living in me that does it.

So I find this law at work: When I want to do good, evil is right there with me. For in my inner being I delight in God's law; but I see another law at work in the members of my body, waging war against the law of my mind and making me a prisoner of the law of sin at work within my members. What a wretched man I am! Who will rescue me from this body of death? Thanks be to God—through Jesus Christ our Lord!

Romans 7:15–25

The third category of suffering is that which comes of being a fallen person. It's the suffering we bring upon ourselves by our own stupidity, our own sinful actions and attitudes. Now this is the category of suffering that makes me nuts! First, because most of my suffering seems to be of this variety. I possess an uncanny ability to bring trouble upon myself. And second, because it's the only category of suffering that we could conceivably minimize, yet I seem bound and determined to *maximize* it. In short, I get on my own nerves.

Yet the reality is we each have our own private "demons," so to speak. Those issues of the heart, habits of mind, and patterns of speaking and acting that cause us to fall short of the glory of God.

One way or another, it all goes back to the Fall. It all goes back to sin, which is simply "falling short of the mark."

We may have the greatest intentions, but how is our follow-through? Although today's passage is long *and* long-winded, it's very comforting to know we're not alone in our humanity. We're not the only ones who mean well but perform poorly. Let's face it, if the apostle Paul—spiritual giant extraordinaire—struggled, what should we expect? I'm currently attending a class called "Train Up a Mom," and this week's homework included a poem by Ruth Bell Graham in which she shares her struggles and frustrations as a mother. As I read it I thought to myself, *If Ruth Graham struggled with motherhood—we're talking about a woman who raised a whole house full of spiritual giants—who am I that I should expect* not *to struggle?*

We're all made of the same stuff: dust. You know what's wonderful, though? God knows it . . . and he loves us *anyway*. This morning I was meditating on Psalm 103 when verses 13 and 14 literally jumped out at me:

> As a father has compassion on his children,
>   so the Lord has compassion on those who fear him;
> for he knows how we are formed,
>   he remembers that we are dust.

I love how Sono Harris[2] puts it, "It's not like God is rolling his eyes at us."

As a child of God, I'm so thankful to know that God isn't rolling his eyes at me every time I blow it, every time I bring needless suffering upon myself and those around me. Yet do I extend the same grace to my own children? This one hit home for me in a big way: I constantly roll my eyes at my kids. Like they are a big disappointment to me. Like I can't *believe* they've fallen short of the mark again. Like it's a big surprise to discover my kids are made of dust, just like me.

So if rolling our eyes at our children's sin isn't the right response, what is?

We cannot spare our children Category #1 suffering. They live in a fallen world. Tornadoes, car wrecks, cancer. We can't prevent those

---

[2]If you're a mother, you simply must order her cassette series called "Martha and Mary." It's available through Christian Book Distributors (CBD). On the web, Christianbook.com.

things from wreaking havoc on our children. We cannot spare our children Category #2 suffering. They live among fallen people. People who will hurt them deeply. Yes, we can shelter them from *some people* for a season, and we should educate them in the fine art of recognizing and fleeing from dangerous people. But they may very well grow up and set their love upon someone who doesn't love them back. They'll have unreasonable bosses. They'll have so-called friends who turn their backs and walk away. It's inevitable. We can't prevent it.

It seems to me that, if we would spare our children suffering, we must focus our attention on Category #3. I believe God has certain lessons for each of us to learn. Now, we can learn the easy way, sitting at his feet, delighting in his Word, and savoring the love he has for us. Or we can learn it the hard way, out there in the cold, cruel world. The more we can get our children to sit at the feet of Jesus, the more lessons they'll learn the *easy way*.

Now, if I could just get their mom to sit at the feet of Jesus and learn the easy way, we'd be in business!

Stand at the Crossroads and Look:

1. Do you tend to bring suffering upon yourself? How?

2. What are some of your "issues of the heart, habits of mind, and patterns of speaking and acting" that routinely cause you "to fall short of the glory of God"? List some of them.

3. How can being alert to these weaknesses help you to minimize Category #3 suffering?

4. Are you relieved to hear that God isn't "rolling his eyes at you"? Who have you been "rolling your eyes at"? How can you get a more compassionate attitude toward that person?

5. What are some life lessons you hope to teach your children the easy way, so they don't have to learn the hard way (perhaps like *you* did)?

6. Write out a prayer in response to today's lesson.

7. What key lesson did you glean from today's study?

Truths to Stand Upon:

- We all have issues of the heart, habits of mind, and patterns of speaking and acting that cause us to fall short of the glory of God.
- God doesn't "roll his eyes" at us; he has compassion on our human frailties.

Day Four

Suffering for a Little While

And the God of all grace, who called you to his eternal glory in Christ, after you have suffered a little while, will himself restore you and make you strong, firm and steadfast. To him be the power for ever and ever. Amen.

1 Peter 5:10–11

Suffering that is ordained by God always has an ultimate purpose, for God's glory and our own good. Naturally, it's often difficult to see the purpose when we're in the thick of things. But it is there. When faced with God's call to suffer for a season, Christians don't always get it right. Oftentimes, we want to flee the suffering, to extricate ourselves from painful situations. That's a normal human reaction, and frankly, I think God designed us that way. We long for the restoration this passage speaks of. We realize, deep within, that the goal is for us to become "strong, firm and steadfast." We're just in too much of a hurry to get there!!! That's why we've spent the first three days of this week talking about the importance of embracing a season of suffering. The truths I have shared thus far weren't novel. You could hear them on any given Sunday, in any given church, on any street corner in America.

Today, I want to shift gears a bit and present a different—perhaps even radical—perspective on the topic of suffering. You've no doubt heard the example of the butterfly, how it struggles to break free from the cocoon and how that process is a vital part of strengthening its wings. The struggle itself makes the butterfly "strong, firm and steadfast." Watching the creature struggle, it's tempting to intervene. We want to ease the suffering and help it to break free. Big mistake. If the butterfly emerges prematurely, without having endured the struggle, its wings will never take flight. It will never fulfill the purpose for which God created it.

But, eventually it must emerge from the struggle. Let me say that again: *Eventually it must emerge from the struggle.* The struggle is not an end in itself. The struggle is the means to an end.

Some Christians have a martyr complex. They are "into" suffering for suffering's sake. I should know. I used to be the Queen of the Martyrs. But suffering for suffering's sake is not ordained by God. It doesn't glorify him, it doesn't make us more effective ministers of the Gospel, and it doesn't advance his Kingdom.

I remember the day God got me by the scruff of the neck and said, essentially, "Listen, girl. I have martyrs all over this globe. There are more people dying for the Gospel right now than at any other time in human history. If I had created you for martyrdom, you would be living in China. Or the Middle East. Or the Sudan. Places where *real* martyrs are enduring *real* suffering for the advance of the Kingdom. You are not a martyr. You are a foolish woman."

Ouch.

So there is a time to emerge from suffering, "after you have suffered a little while." But how long is a little while?

Good question. Wish I knew the answer. Obviously, it is different for every situation. The only way to discern God's timing is to listen intently for God's voice, and here's the key: *Watch intently for his work of restoration to begin.* This passage tells us plainly, God "will himself restore you." It's something God must do. We can't rush it, but we can resist it.

A life of eternal struggle and strife does *not* glorify God, and it does *not* work for our good. It causes non-believers around us to scratch their heads and think, "Well, if that's what serving God is all about, count me out." And it leaves us crippled, deformed creatures, unable to take flight, unable to fulfill the purposes of God for our lives.

But why would we resist restoration? Why would we continue suffering after God declares "a little while" is up? As I've already said, some of us sorta like suffering. We're used to it. It feels familiar, comfortable. But typically, it's because we feel powerless, powerless to change our situation or ourselves. We've become so hopeless, we can't even find the strength to struggle against the obstacle. So we stay trapped in the cocoon and die of suffocation. Or we think we just can't find the energy for that one final push that would enable us to break free. But this verse declares, "to *him* be the power for ever and ever." God does have the power, and the authority, to make radical changes in our lives. And believe it or not, sometimes those changes are *for the better!* Sometimes God says, "My child, you have suffered long enough."

Now some of us just can't hear him speak those words. We have brought the suffering upon ourselves (Category #3), and so we feel we must endure the consequences forever. In our minds, "a little while" surely means a thousand years.

I remember talking with a woman who has been married to a violently abusive alcoholic for thirty-five years. He has sent her to the emergency room so many times she has lost count. She has sustained countless permanent injuries from the beatings, including being completely deaf in her left ear. But she stays and she suffers. And she reeks of bitterness. She says she's a "testimony" to her neighbors. I doubt that's what the neighbors say. As we talked, I gently suggested that perhaps God would release her from such suffering, that perchance her "little while" was up and it was time to move on. I spoke very kindly to her, because I, too, have been a battered wife, so I had great compassion on her situation. As she walked away, I knew she disagreed with me, but I prayed that she would consider the truths I had shared.

Quite the contrary. It turns out, she was absolutely furious with me. In fact, she raised such an outcry against me with the organization hosting the event that they have "banished" me from ever ministering among them again. They even called my publisher to complain about my "radical ideas" and got me into trouble like you wouldn't believe. Well, maybe you would believe it.

Does this sound like a woman whom God has called to a season of suffering for his glory and her own good? Is she becoming more like Christ? Is God being glorified? To glorify God means "to give an accurate reflection" of who he is. Is this portrayal accurate? Does God really want his children to endure this type of indignity for thirty-five years? Could not the mercy of Jesus extend to a situation like this? If Jesus could pardon the thief on the cross, couldn't he pardon this precious child of his? Does God really want his daughters used as punching bags? I used to believe that. I don't anymore.

Does he want his children becoming bitter old women? I don't think so. I once read a poem that said, "A bitter old person is one of the crowning works of the devil." If your suffering is making you bitter, rather than better, you may just need an attitude adjustment (which is what we talked about during the first three days of this week). But then again, maybe it's *past time* for you to emerge. Maybe it's time you allowed God "himself [to] restore you and make you strong, firm and steadfast. To him be the power for ever and ever. Amen."

Stand at the Crossroads and Look:

1. How do you respond to suffering? Do you try to flee and cut it short? Or do you actually prolong it?

2. Have you set yourself up as a martyr? Are you "suffering for suffering's sake"?

3. How do you respond to my contention that God does not ordain "suffering for suffering's sake"? That God only calls us to suffer for a purpose?

4. Is it possible that God is speaking to you when he says, "My child, you have suffered long enough"?

5. Write out a prayer asking God to show you how to respond to your suffering: Is it time to embrace your suffering? Or time to emerge?

6. What key lesson did you glean from today's study?

Truths to Stand Upon:

- Suffering that is ordained by God always has an ultimate purpose, for God's glory and our own good.
- Suffering for suffering's sake does *not* glorify God.
- Eventually, we must emerge from the struggle. The struggle is only a means to an end.
- Sometimes God says, "My child, you have suffered long enough."

Day Five

Stop the Bleeding

Then he said to her, "Daughter, your faith has healed you. Go in peace."

Luke 8:48

I didn't feel like going to church today. First of all, it always means finding clean clothes to wear and battling with my hair. We're talking a two-hour ordeal right there. Second, and more to the point, I had important work to do for the Kingdom of God. Namely, writing this book, and frankly, I felt like I was on a roll, what with all the "novel" and "radical" insights I managed to come up with for yesterday's lesson. But God convicted me about "not forsaking the gathering together, as some are in the habit of doing" (Hebrews 10:25; that's the downside of Scripture memory—it gives God stuff to work with). So off I went to church.

You won't believe what my pastor spoke about. Yep. Suffering. Isn't God awesome??? Not only did he talk about suffering, but he also picked up right where I left off with yesterday's lesson, which I actually wrote this morning, before I agreed with God about getting ready for church. (Gee, am I confusing you?) So, basically, I'm plagiarizing his sermon[3] even as you read these words!

The message was based on Luke 8:42–48, which follows:

> As Jesus was on his way, the crowds almost crushed him. And a woman was there who had been subject to bleeding for twelve years, but no one could heal her. She came up behind him and touched the edge of his cloak, and immediately her bleeding stopped.

---

[3]My thanks to Pastor Gary Knight for the inspiring message.

"Who touched me?" Jesus asked.

When they all denied it, Peter said, "Master, the people are crowding and pressing against you."

But Jesus said, "Someone touched me; I know that power has gone out from me."

Then the woman, seeing that she could not go unnoticed, came trembling and fell at his feet. In the presence of all the people, she told why she had touched him and how she had been instantly healed. Then he said to her, "Daughter, your faith has healed you. Go in peace."

First, our pastor pointed out that Jesus didn't just comfort her in the midst of her suffering. He STOPPED THE BLEEDING. He didn't reassure her that suffering was building her character. He stopped the bleeding. He didn't probe to see whether or not she was to blame, if she "brought it upon herself." He stopped the bleeding. Her "little while" had lasted twelve years before Jesus finally intervened and said, "My child, you have suffered long enough. Be healed. Go in peace." Notice he didn't say, "Stay in peace." He said, "*Go* in peace." Ecclesiastes 3:1 reminds us: "There is a time for everything, and a season for every activity under heaven." There is even "a time to heal" (Ecclesiastes 3:3).

Second, he noted that she didn't let an entire crowd of people keep her away from Jesus. She didn't let them stand between her and the healing she so desperately needed. And yet, we often let *one person* stand between us and the healing Jesus offers. Wow. I wish my pastor would stop reading my prayer journal.

Third, he noted that many people had tried to heal her, but they had all failed. Only Jesus could stop the bleeding. Maybe you've tried to find healing. Maybe you've been to doctors, counselors, pastors, or other experts. But you didn't find the answers you were looking for; you didn't find healing. This woman didn't give up until she got healed. You shouldn't give up either.

Finally, he observed that the woman thought she could go unnoticed. That's probably because she *always* went unnoticed. But Jesus noticed her and cared about her suffering. Maybe you feel unnoticed, like no one sees or cares about your suffering. Jesus sees. He cares.

He wants to stop the bleeding.

Next came the altar call. He asked, "Are you bleeding today? Are you bleeding physically? Are you bleeding emotionally? Maybe you're bleeding financially. Maybe your relationships are broken and bleeding. God wants to stop the bleeding today."

Guess who was the first woman at the altar?

Will you follow me there? Will you mount your courage, muster your faith, and reach out to touch Jesus? Will you let him stop the bleeding?

Stand at the Crossroads and Look:

1. In what way have you been bleeding?

2. Will you allow Jesus to stop the bleeding?

3. Write out a prayer expressing your faith that Jesus is able to heal you, that he is about to stop the bleeding.

4. What key lesson did you glean from today's study?

5. Write out This Week's Verse from memory.

Truths to Stand Upon:

- There is a time for everything, even a time to heal.
- Jesus wants to heal us and "stop the bleeding."

Weekly Review:

Take a few moments to fill in the ten actions and attitudes required to Stand Firm. Look in the back of the book if you need help.

S _____ God first

S _____ God's perspective

S _____ your spiritual hunger

S _____ the love God has for you

S _____ yourself against the attacks of the enemy

S _____ truth to yourself and others

S _____ the tide of mediocrity

S _____ like a saint

S _____ wholeheartedly

S _____ firm until the end

WEEK NINE:
Serve Wholeheartedly

This Week's Verse:

Therefore, thus says the Lord,
"If you return, then I will restore you—
Before Me you will stand;
And if you extract the precious from the worthless,
You will become My spokesman."

Jeremiah 15:19 (NASB)

Day One

Extracting the Precious

Therefore, thus says the Lord,
"If you return, then I will restore you—
Before Me you will stand;
And if you extract the precious from the worthless.
You will become My spokesman."

Jeremiah 15:19 (NASB)

Much has been said, in this book and many others, about what it takes to be a servant of Christ. Some say we must be role models. Get our families with the program and keep our spices in alphabetical order. Have an answer for everything. Put a smile on our face and always "be ready to give a reason for the hope that we have" (1 Peter 3:15). Good witnesses don't have bad days. When those around us observe how amazing we are, how our husband is a captain of industry and our son is the captain of the football team, they'll want to know "what we have" so they can bow the knee and pray the prayer.

I guess you can sense my skepticism, huh? I want to acknowledge right here and now, it's entirely possible that this approach to Christianity and evangelism *works*. It's entirely possible that there are, in fact, Christians out there who are such incredible testimonies, such shining lights, that people respond in droves.

The problem is, I just haven't met any of them.

Given the condition of my own life, it's possible that these wonderful Christians do, in fact, exist; they just don't want to associate with the likes of me. Lately, I've been pondering the notion that there's an entire subculture comprised of dynamic, victorious Christians. No, I'm serious. They really *could* be out there somewhere. I envision them gathering for Bible studies and holiday celebrations. I envision their beautiful houses, happy marriages, and obedient children. I sure wish they'd invite me to the party.

Meanwhile, back at the ranch, I've grappled to find my place in the Kingdom. It ain't in the upper echelon, that's for sure. Does God have any use for someone like me? Today's verse offers hope that he does:

> Therefore, thus says the Lord,
> "If you return, then I will restore you—
> Before Me you will stand;
> And if you extract the precious from the worthless,
> You will become My spokesman." (Jeremiah 15:19, NASB)

The passage is speaking to someone who has wandered away. Okay, done that. Someone in need of restoration. That would be me. Someone struggling to stand. Check. Someone who has endured seemingly worthless experiences. Okay, *that's it! Jeremiah, stop talking about me!*

God offers someone like me—someone like you?—an incredible opportunity: to become his spokesman. If. Notice the word *if*. If we will *extract* the precious from all the worthless stuff we've endured, then we'll have something to say that people need to hear. Writing in his book *A Farewell to Arms*, Ernest Hemingway observed that "the world breaks everyone, and afterward many are strong at the broken places."

In Eastern Europe there is a factory that crafts exquisite vases that sell for thousands of dollars. They have a fascinating technique. First, their potters spin clay into almost paper-thin vases. The vase is so fragile that if you "ding" it with your finger, it will break. If there is the slightest flaw in the design, the vase is immediately discarded. If the vase is flawless, it's turned over to an artist who delicately paints a one-of-a-kind work of art on the surface. When the artist is finished, he lovingly holds up his masterpiece—and drops it into a large metal box. It smashes into hundreds of tiny pieces.

Then another workman comes along and takes the box away. For days, he painstakingly glues the vase back together. But no matter how hard he tries, the vase looks hideously ugly. There's just no way to hide the cracks. The vase is still fragile, though stronger than it was before the glue.

Finally, another artist takes over. This artist works with pounded gold, which he uses to paint over each and every crack on that vase. The result is not only an exquisite work of art—far more beautiful than the original, far more beautiful than it could ever have been if it hadn't been broken—but the vase is so strong, it is virtually unbreakable.

God, the master craftsman, has formed you exactly the way he wanted you to be. You are a masterpiece. He is the potter who formed you from a lump of clay, then painted your skin, your eyes, your lips, your hair. And yes, he is the one who lovingly allowed you to drop momentarily. The one whose heart stopped beating when you smashed to the bottom of that metal box. He is the same one who pulled you from the rubble and painstakingly glued you back together. And he is the master artist who wants not to *hide or conceal* those broken places in your life, but to *accentuate them.* To guild them with gold until they glisten.

It is in the broken places that we are made strong. It is at the broken places that we are made beautiful to behold. Is it your desire to serve God wholeheartedly? Release yourself into his hands. Allow him to make something beautiful from each and every broken place in your life.[1]

Stand at the Crossroads and Look:

1. Respond to the story of the Eastern European vase factory. Describe how you felt as the process unfolded.

---

[1] If you are interested in exploring the concept of "broken places" in greater detail, refer to my previous books, *Living in Absolute Freedom* and *Becoming a Vessel God Can Use.*

2. Have you observed the same process unfolding in your own life?
   Describe.

3. Write out a prayer expressing your desire to "extract the precious
   from the worthless" so that you might become God's spokesman.

4. What key lesson did you glean from today's study?

Truths to Stand Upon:

- The world breaks everyone, and afterward many are strong at the
  broken places.
- God doesn't want to conceal the broken places in your life; he
  wants to accentuate them and transform them into something
  beautiful.

Day Two

Serving the Brokenhearted

The Spirit of the Sovereign Lord is on me,
because the Lord has anointed me
to preach good news to the poor.
He has sent me to bind up the brokenhearted,
to proclaim freedom for the captives
and release from darkness for the prisoners,
to proclaim the year of the Lord's favor
and the day of vengeance of our God,
to comfort all who mourn,
and provide for those who grieve in Zion—
to bestow on them a crown of beauty
instead of ashes,
the oil of gladness
instead of mourning,
and a garment of praise
instead of a spirit of despair.

Isaiah 61:1–3

Today's passage is the Messiah's job description. Jesus came to bind up the brokenhearted. If we would follow after him and serve him wholeheartedly, I believe it must become our job description as well. In my previous book *Living in Absolute Freedom*, I shared how I conclude my retreats with a ceremony of brokenness. I won't recount the entire procedure here, but in the end, I am left standing by an altar filled with broken pieces of clay. Scribbled on those pieces are words describing the broken places of each woman who came forward.

I will often sit and pray over the broken pieces and the broken places they represent. In so doing, I have observed five fundamental areas of brokenness, which cross all geographic and demographic boundaries. These will come as no surprise to anyone who has previously served in ministry. They are:

- Physical Brokenness
- Relational Brokenness
- Spiritual Brokenness
- Sexual Brokenness
- Emotional Brokenness

We will examine each in turn.

Physical Brokenness

I often see the word *cancer* scrawled on the clay. I also see infertility, arthritis, and chronic fatigue. What surprised me was how many women wrote, in essence, "I'm fat and ugly and lazy and I hate myself." However, this shouldn't catch us off guard if we think about it. Our culture exalts thin, beautiful women, and even the church idolizes accomplishment. It's no wonder that the average woman feels inadequate and "less than" everyone else.

It's interesting to note that our culture is well aware that many feel broken in this area. The next time you're in the grocery store checkout line, take a moment to study magazine covers. Believe me, the publishing industry spends millions, probably billions, conducting market research to determine what topics to splatter across the front. I guarantee they are going straight to the "heart of the matter" for a vast majority of American women. Let's learn what we can from them. So think: What issues are they addressing?

Weight loss.

Health.

And beauty.

That's because they've figured out something most churches miss. These are *real concerns* for real people living in the real world. If you're too sick and tired to make it through the day, if you think you're so fat and ugly that you despise yourself, you've got a *real* problem.

Unfortunately, the world has no real solutions to offer. Only Saran Wrap. We must do better. It's not enough for the church to say to women, "Oh, you *shouldn't* care about such superficial stuff." The fact is, women *do* care, and when we tell them they "shouldn't," all we're doing is adding guilt to the mix. Instead, we must "bestow on them a crown of beauty."

How might you minister wholeheartedly to the physical brokenness of the women in your world?

Relational Brokenness

Women have broken marriages. Some have ended in divorce, others are just coexisting in pain and despair. Women have prodigal children, children who are making bad choices or who have wandered from the faith entirely. And women are lonely.

Let's tackle the last one first. Go back to the supermarket checkout stand for a moment. You'll see entire magazines devoted to gossip about movie stars, and even more frightening, about soap opera stars. Why? Because women are broken relationally. And since their real relationships in the real world are shattered, seemingly beyond repair, they try to connect with artificial people in a plastic world.

What a sad commentary on the church. Where are we in the midst of this lonely generation? This is a problem we can *easily* solve. Yet too often, we're traveling around in our little cliques, hosting superficial "fellowship" activities and congratulating ourselves on our moral superiority. And it's not just women outside the church who are lonely. I think it's an absolute disgrace than any woman in the church would feel lonely, but I can tell you from personal experience: Sitting in a pew is often the loneliest place on earth. My sisters, this shouldn't be so. We need to get *real* with one another!

We need to "proclaim freedom for the captives" of loneliness.

How might you minister wholeheartedly to the relational brokenness of lonely women?

What of prodigal children? Here again, the church often does more harm than good. Parents are told, "Listen, just follow this little formula: A+B=C" and you're guaranteed to have great kids who honor and glorify your name. Oops, we mean, glorify God. I actually have a parenting book that, God is my witness, uses precisely this format. There's a formula running throughout the book, and by the time you get to the last chapter, you should have great kids.

Guess what, folks? You can't plug human beings into nice, neat little formulas. You see, Perfect Parent plus Perfect Child does NOT always equal Perfect Adult. Was not God the Perfect Father? Were not Adam and Eve the most Perfect Humans ever created? Did they become Perfect Adults? Not even close.

It all comes back to Saran Wrap, doesn't it?

If we would serve wholeheartedly, we're gonna have to get real. We're gonna have to be honest enough to admit that sometimes our children make terrible choices and that doesn't make us terrible parents. Just human beings. Holding forth magic formulas won't help. Raising our eyebrows with a "well, they mustn't have followed the formula correctly" attitude won't bring healing. Love and compassion will. It's high time we offer "the oil of gladness" to those mourning the painful choices of their wayward children.

Now let's make it personal. How might you minister wholeheartedly to the relational brokenness experienced by the parents of prodigals?

Guess what? There's so much brokenness in the world, we'll have to continue this discussion tomorrow. Meanwhile, ponder the broken places we've shared thus far.

Stand at the Crossroads and Look:

1. How might you minister wholeheartedly to the physical brokenness of the women in your world?

2. How might you minister wholeheartedly to the relational brokenness of lonely women?

3. How might you minister wholeheartedly to the relational broken-ness experienced by the parents of prodigals?

4. Write out a prayer responding to today's lesson.

5. What key lesson did you glean from today's study?

Truths to Stand Upon:

- For those struggling with low self-esteem, we must "bestow on them a crown of beauty."
- We need to "proclaim freedom for the captives" of loneliness.
- We must offer "the oil of gladness" to those mourning the painful choices of their wayward children.

Day Three

Serving the Brokenhearted, Day Two

The Spirit of the Sovereign Lord is on me,
because the Lord has anointed me
to preach good news to the poor.
He has sent me to bind up the brokenhearted,
to proclaim freedom for the captives
and release from darkness for the prisoners,
to proclaim the year of the Lord's favor
and the day of vengeance of our God,
to comfort all who mourn,
and provide for those who grieve in Zion—
to bestow on them a crown of beauty
instead of ashes,
the oil of gladness
instead of mourning,
and a garment of praise
instead of a spirit of despair.   Isaiah 61:1–3

Yesterday, we left off midway through dealing with *Relational Brokenness*. Ready or not, we need to tackle marital brokenness today. It's all around us. We can't wish it away any longer. I recently heard a statistic indicating that the divorce rate *in* the church (sixty-three percent) is actually *higher* than the divorce rate for the general public (sixty percent). My own sense, just from anecdotal evidence, is that this is accurate. Now, it would be tempting to conclude that Christians have gone soft on marriage. That more couples need to "buck up" and "suck up." It's tempting to conclude that divorce is the problem. I don't believe that is the case.

The problem isn't divorce. The problem is the broken marriages that end up in divorce. And if the problem of divorce is rampant in the church, the problem of broken marriages is epidemic. Let's do some basic math here. If sixty-three percent of Christians are so miserable they actually go through with a divorce—setting themselves up for the heartache and stigma that will result—what *additional* percentage of Christians have broken marriages, even though they *are not* getting divorced? Eighty percent? Ninety percent? Scary, isn't it?

Once again, I am willing to concede that my experience is limited. I have not conducted a formal poll or done extensive research. However, I have communicated with thousands of women around the world—in person, through the mail, and over the Internet. And I hear their heart-wrenching stories of marital brokenness. Tales of abuse, adultery, incest, pornography addiction, alcoholism, homosexuality, gambling debt, financial ruin, you name it. If it's happening in the world, it's happening in the church. We're just doing a "better job" of covering up in public.

I know how unpleasant this stuff must be to read about. I wish I could just wave my magic wand and make it all go away. Or break out the Saran Wrap and cover it up. The church has done that far too long, my sisters. It's time to get real. If we would serve wholeheartedly, then we must face these painful truths and be prepared to respond with compassion.

Those of you who've read my previous books know this is a tender spot in my heart. Shortly after becoming a Christian, I became involved with a Middle Eastern Muslim man who took total control of my life. I have shared the story with tens of thousands of people, how God enabled me to endure ten years as a virtual hostage in my own home. I wasn't allowed to leave my house without his permission and strict supervision—not even to walk around the block or sit on the front steps.

Although I never stated it outright, I assume most readers and listeners were able to put two and two together and conclude the obvious: I was a battered woman. What I wasn't permitted to share was just how awful my life continued to be, even after I was "allowed" to journey much farther than the corner store.

I loved the Lord with all my heart and found great joy in serving him. Nevertheless, my marriage was broken. I read marriage books, attended marriage seminars, listened to marriage tapes, and attended Bible studies on becoming a better wife. But my marriage was still broken. I turned that broken place over to God and asked him to guild it with gold, to transform it into something beautiful. I would stand before audiences and hold up my broken piece of clay, declaring publicly, "Father, I gave this broken piece to you. Redeem it. Use it anyway you can for the advance of your Kingdom." And I meant that sincerely.

But do you know what I whispered under my breath each time? "Father, you can use the brokenness of my marriage anyway you choose *as long as it all works out in the end and as long as I look good in the process.*"

I have managed to avoid this subject for nine weeks of our journey. I can avoid it no longer. It grieves me to tell you this. First and foremost, because I know it will grieve many of you. You will be disappointed in me. Some of you will reject me. You will put this book down and vow never to read anything else that I write. You may drop out of the class right now. If you have been reading this, considering whether or not to teach it this spring or fall, you may choose a "safer" book instead.

But you have a right to know, and so I have an obligation to tell you: My marriage has ended in divorce.

Tempted though I am to stand on the highest mountain and recount for all the world every detail of how "he done me wrong," I think the most God-honoring thing is to simply say this: I did the best I could to make my broken marriage succeed. Instead, it failed.

My husband became involved in a "situation" that nearly destroyed me emotionally and psychologically. Nevertheless, I was strongly urged to forgive and forget. We reconciled for a few months, but I eventually came to the place where I simply could not live another day with the painful consequences of his choices. Perhaps a stronger Christian would have worked harder to restore the marriage. Perhaps a woman of greater faith would have held out for a miracle. But I am telling you, my precious sisters, from the brokenness of my heart: I had nothing left to give. When I originally wrote this, I was careful to point out that *he* filed the divorce papers. I was even sure to mention the date he filed. I wanted to let myself off the hook. I wanted to point the finger at him and make sure he took all the blame. But that was really disingenuous, because the truth is he filed only after he realized I had completely given up hope. I'm not proud of my weakness, but God's grace has truly been sufficient.

Someone recently asked me if I thought divorce was a sin. Specifically, she wanted to know if I felt that I had sinned. The answer is, obviously, yes. Any time we fall short of the mark, we have sinned. We are all sinners, saved only by the grace and mercy of God. I know one thing for certain: I have never been more thankful for the Cross—and the atoning blood that was shed there. Through my divorce recovery process, God has tenderly shown me the dreadful condition of my heart, how I had become consumed with sin, especially anger, resentment, and bitterness—the kind of pernicious sins that destroy a person from the inside out. It's been painful to confront the truth, but also tremendously healing. Although I'm not happy that my children and I have had to endure the pain of divorce, I'm happy to report that it has driven us to our knees. I find that I am becoming more and more like Jesus, and less and less like the self-congratulatory stone thrower I once was. More inclined to bake a casserole, less inclined to inquire whether or not there were "grounds."

I have experienced the ultimate marital brokenness. And all the Saran Wrap in the world won't fix it. No wave of the magic wand can heal it. I am a divorced woman. I am the woman down the street. I am the woman in the pew next to you.

I believe Christ is calling us "to comfort all who mourn, and provide for those who grieve in Zion." I believe divorced women deserve the same love and support we would extend to a widow. Perhaps you are shocked to hear me say that. Perhaps even angry. But I believe it with all my heart. Both have experienced a devastating loss. Both are grieving. It benefits no one for us to sit around with a moral calculator, trying to assess what percentage of blame the woman deserves for the collapse of her marriage and then portion out assistance accordingly. If she seems even remotely to blame, she gets *no help, no love, no compassion.*

A dear friend of mine, a pastor's wife whose husband had an affair with a teenage girl, was told by another pastor: "If a man runs to another woman, his wife should look in the mirror to find out why." I find it impossible to imagine Jesus uttering such contemptuous words. Although most of us would never say such a thing, do our actions communicate the same attitude?

If you would serve wholeheartedly, how would you respond to a woman whose marriage is relationally broken? A woman who is struggling or whose marriage has ended in divorce? How would you respond to a woman . . . like me?

Stand at the Crossroads and Look:

1. Have you observed marital brokenness? What has been its effect on those involved?

2. Have you experienced some degree of marital brokenness? How has it affected you? Those around you?

3. How does your church respond to those suffering marital brokenness?

4. Do you believe the response is appropriate? Why or why not?

5. Would you write out a prayer . . . for me?

6. What key lesson did you glean from today's study?

Truths to Stand Upon:

- Christ is calling us "to comfort all who mourn, and provide for those who grieve in Zion."
- Divorced women deserve the same love and support we would extend to a widow. They are both grieving a devastating loss.

Day Four

Serving the Brokenhearted, Day Three

The Spirit of the Sovereign Lord is on me,
*   because the Lord has anointed me*
*   to preach good news to the poor.*
He has sent me to bind up the brokenhearted,
*   to proclaim freedom for the captives*
*   and release from darkness for the prisoners,*
to proclaim the year of the Lord's favor
*   and the day of vengeance of our God,*
to comfort all who mourn,
*   and provide for those who grieve in Zion—*
to bestow on them a crown of beauty
*   instead of ashes,*
the oil of gladness
*   instead of mourning,*
and a garment of praise
*   instead of a spirit of despair.*   Isaiah 61:1–3

Spiritual Brokenness

"I've stopped going to church." "I feel far from God." "I'm afraid God is angry with me." These are the areas of spiritual brokenness I encounter, which typically are an outgrowth of the other areas of brokenness. Perhaps a woman became swept up into a set of circumstances that led her into a "serious sin." One woman told me how she had become enthralled with a man who professed to be a Christian, but turned out to be a con man of the first order. Because she was madly in love with him, she become involved in his various criminal schemes. Of course, all sin is serious in God's eyes, but we tend to classify. Gossip is no big deal. Stealing? That's a big one. So she hid from God, just like Adam and Eve did in the Garden after committing the first sin. Now she's struggling to find her way back home.

I'm thinking of another woman whose church disappointed her in a profound way. The pastor embezzled funds from the church, then he and the church secretary abandoned their spouses and ran off together with the money. The entire congregation was devastated and disillusioned. So she drifted away.

Another woman became involved with a church that was cultish in its practices—controlling, rigid, judgmental, and just plain "off the wall." When she finally woke up and realized how far afield that particular church was, it turned her off to the church as a whole.

I meet countless women who have fallen victim to "church politics," gossip and backbiting, or who have endured some other personal offense, and they've clung to it for years. As a result, they have fallen out of fellowship, lost accountability, and—as one might expect—their spiritual life has suffered as a result.

Some women have "wandered from the faith and pierced themselves with many griefs" (1 Timothy 6:10) for no apparent reason whatsoever. These cases are the hardest to handle. I'll never forget one woman who told me she was raised in a pastor's home and grew up to marry a pastor. Her dad was great; her husband was great; even her kids were great. Life was wonderful. In a moment that can only be described as sheer madness, she picked up the newspaper and turned to the Personal Ads. There she discovered a man looking for a "discreet" relationship. She responded. They began an affair, which eventually led to the collapse of her marriage. (Three choices away from destruction.)

She literally had no one to blame but herself. This man didn't con her. No childhood or marital abuse set her up to become a victim. She knew exactly what she was getting herself into, and she did it anyway. She was, perhaps, the most unsympathetic prodigal I had ever encountered. Yet that's precisely why my heart broke for her, and why I remember her so vividly to this day.

We talked about the cross. We talked about how Jesus died for every incredibly stupid choice we've ever made. He died for those who don't deserve forgiveness. He even died for those who were born to spiritual privilege and willingly chose to throw away their inheritance.

We cried together. And we prayed together. I hope she's doing okay.

I meet many women who have simply gotten caught up in the busyness of life and made God number twenty-seven on their priority list. Frankly, I suspect that's the most common cause. But it matters not the cause. God wants to heal all spiritual brokenness. Through our healing hearts and hands, he wants to offer "a garment of praise instead of a spirit of despair."

If we would serve wholeheartedly, we must extend grace and mercy to the prodigal, however far from home she may have journeyed.

Sexual Brokenness

I recently spoke at a Christian writer's conference, and my advice to attendees who wanted to write about sexual brokenness was simple: self-publish. Rare indeed is the publishing house willing to touch the subject. Rare indeed is the *church* willing to touch the subject. Yet as I kneel at altars across America, I gaze upon broken piece after broken piece scribbled with: adultery, abortion, molestation, incest, and rape.[2] Weekend after weekend, these are among the *most common* words I read. I've yet to encounter "sexual dysfunction," but my guess is it's rampant as well.

Research indicates that one in four American women has been sexually abused the the age of eighteen.

Think about it for a second. It is likely that every one of you has either experienced some form of sexual dysfunction or knows someone who has. Incredible. Heartbreaking. Depressing. The problems are enormous, the challenge is immense. Bethany House Publishers has been one of the few brave enough to publish a number of great resources:

- *Sexual Assault: Will I Ever Feel Okay Again?*—Kay Scott
- *Helping Women Recover from Abortion*—Nancy Michels

---

[2] One of the exercises I use during my retreats is to have the women break clay pots and write their deepest sins and struggles on the broken pieces. These pieces are then placed on an altar where we pray over them and ask God to re-create us into vessels that he can use for his glory.

- *Counseling the Homosexual*—Mike Saia
- *Family Under Siege*—George Grant
- *Helping the Victims of Sexual Abuse*—Lynn Heitritter and Jeanette Vought
- *Good News for the Chemically Dependent and Those Who Love Them*—Jeff VanVonderen

Just this past Thursday at our weekly Bible study, one of the women began weeping as she asked us to pray for a little boy named Bobby. She had met him when she worked at a home for wayward children. Bobby's grandparents had kept him locked in a closet for nine years. The only time they let him out was when they wanted to sexually abuse him. Bobby was eventually rescued from that nightmare, but the nightmarish consequences are still playing out in his life. Bobby's behavior was so outrageous that he had to be removed from the group home. My friend has lost track of him. He's out there somewhere, broken and in desperate need of a Savior. We prayed that God would send someone to help him. Would you be one to say, "Here I am, Lord. Send me to Bobby."

To those who have endured the unspeakable, God is calling us to speak words of healing. He's calling us "to comfort all who mourn, . . . to bestow on them a crown of beauty instead of ashes, the oil of gladness instead of mourning, and a garment of praise instead of a spirit of despair."

If we would serve wholeheartedly, we must force ourselves to gaze upon the brokenness wrought by some of the darkest deeds human beings are capable of. It won't be pretty. It won't be as fun as hosting a tea party. And not everyone has the courage to do it. But it is time for some among us to step forward in wholehearted service to those shattered by sexual brokenness.

Stand at the Crossroads and Look:

1. Are you struggling with an area of spiritual brokenness? What is the root cause?

2. What practical steps can you take to begin healing your spiritual brokenness?

3. Are you aware of someone else who is struggling with spiritual brokenness? Someone who has fallen away from the faith? Or from fellowship/church attendance?

4. How can you reach out to restore that prodigal?

5. Have you suffered sexual brokenness? In what way?

6. What steps to healing might you need to take?

7. Is it possible that God is calling you to minister to those suffering from sexual brokenness? How so?

8. Write out a prayer asking God to heal you in these areas of brokenness *and* to make you a channel of healing for others who are still struggling.

9. What key lesson did you glean from today's study?

Truths to Stand Upon:

- If we would serve wholeheartedly, we must extend grace and mercy to the prodigal, however far from home she may have journeyed.
- If we would serve wholeheartedly, we must force ourselves to gaze upon the brokenness wrought by some of the darkest deeds human beings are capable of.

Day Five

Serving the Brokenhearted, Day Four

The Spirit of the Sovereign Lord is on me,
because the Lord has anointed me
to preach good news to the poor.
He has sent me to bind up the brokenhearted,
to proclaim freedom for the captives
and release from darkness for the prisoners,
to proclaim the year of the Lord's favor
and the day of vengeance of our God,
to comfort all who mourn,
and provide for those who grieve in Zion—
to bestow on them a crown of beauty
instead of ashes,
the oil of gladness
instead of mourning,
and a garment of praise
instead of a spirit of despair.   Isaiah 61:1–3

Emotional Brokenness

We can write it off to PMS, I suppose. The fact remains, however, that there are a huge number of Christian women struggling with depression, anger, and other out-of-control emotions. In some cases, the cause is physical. Their biochemistry has gotten out of whack somehow, perhaps from the birth of a child, entering a new phase of life like menopause, or a dramatic change in their circumstances or environment. We live in jars of clay, after all. And some jars are more easily shattered than others.

Some emotional problems are rooted in poor diet and lack of

exercise. It begins with a bag of Oreos which sends your serotonin[3] levels plummeting, your insulin levels skyrocketing, and your fat cells expanding. Next thing you know, the scales are tipping past 150 pounds and you can't fit into any of your clothes. Just thinking about it is enough to makedepressed. So the downward spiral begins, and you feel powerless to get back up. Been there big time.

I've openly admitted that I've struggled with depression my whole life, and that my biochemistry seemed to have permanently run amok. I knew that my shattered biochemistry was causing the frequent plunges into despair. I knew it wasn't enough for me to "read my Bible and pray more" as so many Christians suggested I should do. I knew depression was a real illness, rooted in physical causes. And it is.

I'm only now beginning to understand that the cycle works both ways: Your *emotions* impact your biochemistry, just as much as your biochemistry affects your emotions. Talk about your vicious cycles! YIKES!!! The emotional trauma of my childhood, compounded by twenty years spent suffering from Battered Wife Syndrome, had taken a toll on my body and my biochemistry, leaving me vulnerable to emotional ups and downs. So much so that I was wrongly diagnosed as suffering from bipolar disorder.

In the final years of my marriage, I was so overwhelmed with despair, I was sleeping an average of twelve hours per day. Shocked? Then you've never suffered from depression. Ironically, even though these past two years have been extremely painful, and Lord knows I've cried more than my share of tears, I have not experienced even one bout with depression. Grief? Yes. Discouragement? Yes. But not that hopeless, bottomless pit of depression.

Although life as a single parent is challenging, I wake up first thing in the morning ready to face those challenges with God's help. I actually *get out of bed* willingly. Now most of you are thinking, "What's the big deal? Doesn't everyone get out of bed?" For me, and anyone else who has struggled with depression, it is a HUGE deal. I mean to tell you, it's a brand new experience in my life!

Perhaps some of you will remember the old praise chorus:

---

[3]Serotonin is a chemical in the brain that controls your sense of well-being. It's a proven fact that this chemical fluctuates in direct relation to your diet.

I woke up this morning with my mind stayed on Jesus
I woke up this morning with my mind stayed on Jesus
I woke up this morning with my mind stayed on Jesus.
Hallelu. Hallelu. Hallelujah.

Well, thanks to a recent lecture I heard by Antoinette Dawson, I have now adopted this as my inspirational morning motto. Let's take it apart. First, "I woke up this morning." Now, that's a start, isn't it? I remember many mornings when I just couldn't wake up. Besides, at the risk of sounding morose, there are people all over the world who literally won't wake up today. So, hey, if you woke up this morning you are ahead of the game.

Let's see. Next. "With my mind." EXCELLENT. I am continually on the verge of losing my mind, so if I wake up and discover, "Yes, my mind is still functioning, at least on some level," then I'm doubly grateful. I meet lots of crazy people in my travels, so I venture to say that if you woke up this morning with your mind, you can consider yourself well above average.

"Stayed on Jesus." Listen, there are a lot worse things my mind can drift toward. When I recently sang this song for a sweet group of ladies, I had to admit that I had woke up that particular morning with my mind stayed on this really hot guy at the gym. Since that's not an entirely unusual occurrence, I figure any morning when I wake up with my mind headed in the right direction, I've got something to be thankful for!

Well, enough silliness. Let's get back to the issue of emotional brokenness. I'm no expert, but I'll tell you this much: I believe the key to my healing has been forgiveness. (And the key to forgiving was getting to a place where it was safe to forgive—a place where forgiving did not equal enabling or facilitating sin.) Now I'm going to say something that would have made me angry if someone had said it to me two years ago: I think all emotional brokenness is rooted in unforgiveness. I'll go one further: I think *the power behind* ALL brokenness is rooted in unforgiveness. Stop and think. The POWER BEHIND all brokenness is rooted in unforgiveness.

You may be suffering from cancer, but if you've forgiven God for allowing it to come into your life, and/or you've forgiven the doctor for not catching it sooner, and you've forgiven *yourself* for smoking, not getting a mammogram, breathing, or whatever else you've been beating yourself up for, then *it has no power over you.*

You may feel fat and ugly, but if you've forgiven your mom for passing on her lousy body type and for teaching you that food is the ultimate reward, and you've forgiven your husband for not making enough money so you can hire a personal trainer, and you've forgiven yourself for being a less-than-perfect human being, then *it has no power over you.*

You may have endured a broken relationship. But if you've forgiven your child for wandering away, for being a disappointment to you; and you've forgiven your husband for failing to be Prince Charming; and you've forgiven yourself for your part in the whole sorry mess, then *it has no power over you.*

Maybe you are experiencing spiritual brokenness. But if you've forgiven the people you think drove you away from God, and if you've forgiven yourself for walking away, then *it has no power over you.*

You may even have endured the horror of sexual brokenness. But if you can find it within yourself to forgive the person who violated you and you can forgive yourself for any false guilt and self-blame you've carried, then *it has no power over you.*

I firmly believe that if you can find a way to forgive those who've hurt you—and harder still—find a way to forgive yourself, you will not remain emotionally broken. You will begin to heal. *I am living proof.*

One elderly woman shared with me how she had struggled all her life to forgive her brother. Then one day as she was praying, God gave her a vision of how *he* saw her brother. He was a severely crippled, shriveled up old man who could barely walk down the street. Suddenly, she realized the truth of her brother's spiritual handicap. And she was able to forgive him.

This past year, I worked through Neil T. Anderson's outstanding book *Bondage Breaker*, in which he includes an exercise in forgiveness. You make a list of all the people who have hurt you, then forgive them one by one. Let me tell you, I had a looooooooooong list. And I was broken in every way that a person could be broken. As I began to pray, God showed me over and over:

He was just an idiot.
She didn't know any better.
He did the best he could.
She hurt you because she was hurting.

As I read name after name on the list and recalled the pain each one had inflicted, I couldn't believe how *easy* it was to forgive. And then I got to my own name and I realized:

I was just an idiot.
I didn't know any better.
I did the best I could.
I let people hurt me because I was hurting.
I hurt people because I was hurting.

God wants us "to preach good news to the poor" and that includes the poor woman in the mirror. He wants us to "bind up the broken-hearted" and that includes the brokenhearted woman in the mirror. He wants us "to proclaim freedom for the captives" and that includes the captive woman in the mirror. He wants us to "release prisoners" from the darkness of depression and that includes the prisoner in the mirror. He wants us "to proclaim the year of the Lord's favor" and that favor extends—yes, it extends even to the woman in the mirror.

If we would serve wholeheartedly, we must begin by forgiving ourselves and others.

Stand at the Crossroads and Look:

1. Have you suffered from emotional brokenness? In what way?

2. Make a list of everyone who has hurt or offended you in your life. Use a separate page, if you would feel more comfortable with that.

3. Set aside at least an hour to pray through your list, asking God to help you forgive each person.

4. Write out a prayer expressing the truths God showed you as you prayed through your list.

5. What key lesson did you glean from today's study?

6. Write out This Week's Verse from memory.

Truths to Stand Upon:

- The power behind all brokenness is unforgiveness.
- If we would serve wholeheartedly, we must begin by forgiving ourselves and others.

Weekly Review:

Take a few moments to fill in the ten actions and attitudes required to Stand Firm. Look in the back of the book if you need help.

S _____ God first

S _____ God's perspective

S _____ your spiritual hunger

S _____ the love God has for you

S _____ yourself against the attacks of the enemy

S _____ truth to yourself and others

S _____ the tide of mediocrity

S _____ like a saint

S _____ wholeheartedly

S _____ firm until the end

WEEK TEN:
Stand Firm Until the End

This Week's Verse:

Some trust in chariots and some in horses,
but we trust in the name of the Lord our God.
They are brought to their knees and fall,
but we rise up and stand firm.

Psalm 20:7–8

Day One

A Place to Stand

May he give you the desire of your heart
and make all your plans succeed.
We will shout for joy when you are victorious
and will lift up our banners in the name of our God.
May the Lord grant all your requests.
Now I know that the Lord saves his anointed;
he answers him from his holy heaven
with the saving power of his right hand.
Some trust in chariots and some in horses,
but we trust in the name of the Lord our God.
They are brought to their knees and fall,
but we rise up and stand firm.   Psalm 20:4–8

I assume you took time this morning to carefully read today's verse, but I'd encourage you to go back and pray through it again. It goes to the heart of standing firm. It speaks with absolute confidence that God takes care of his children. Since God is able to deliver completely those whose hope is in him, we can walk through all the days of our lives with total God-Confidence. God-Confidence is the absolute assurance that God can do whatever he wants through whomever he chooses.

This morning as I was getting dressed for church, I got to thinking about God and his saving power in my life. It occurred to me that God knew, even before I was born, the pain I would suffer and the stupid choices I would make along the way. He knew I would become a "rejection junkie" who deliberately tries to push people out of her life. He knew I would become not only a drug addict, but a drug dealer as well. He knew I would enter an ill-advised marriage to a Muslim man. And he knew that after twenty years of struggle, I would finally admit the truth: I had no business entering into such a relationship in the first place. I tried to tell myself that God was "entrusting" me with suffering because I was such a spiritual giant, like Job the faithful servant. No, my suffering had nothing to do with my faithfulness and everything to do with my folly. It's frightening how we can deceive ourselves. Yet God knew in advance how deceitful my heart would be. He knew all these things, yet he chose to set his love upon me anyway.

My life is a journey, complete with wrong turns. It's my life; it's not a prescription. It's not the same as yours; it's uniquely mine. We're back to the pink fluorescent T-shirt, aren't we? This is the journey I'm on right now because this is where my life choices have brought me. But also because it's where a sovereign God has allowed me to be. This is my life. On many days, I wish it were someone else's. But it isn't. And I wish someone else could walk it, but they can't. I'm the only one who can wake up every day and face it with all that is within me, by the grace and mercy of God.

Some days I make lousy choices. Or I choose to let life happen to me, which is a choice, too. But I have brighter days when I choose wisely and live rightly. Funny thing is, God loves me exactly the same no matter what kind of day I am having. He loves me in the midst of my real life—the one I am currently living, not the one I ought to live.

I often point out to God that "this is not the life I signed up for." I distinctly remember signing up for the life where everything turned out right, a life where I could trust in "chariots and horses." You know, things that are supposed to be dependable. Chariots like "real Christians never get divorced." And horses like "everything will work out in the end." I've learned not to put my trust in chariots and horses anymore. I've learned to trust in God and God alone. I've discovered that the only place to stand firm is upon his unconditional love. It can't be shaken. It can't be taken from me. I can't even push him away. Lord knows I've tried.

Love isn't unconditional if you have to perform for it, if you have to earn it. It isn't unconditional if you have to watch your back, if you're in constant risk of jeopardizing it. So God's love is settled. I can choose to spend my days in absolute debauchery—drinking, drugs, sleeping around—it won't shake his love for me. I'm free to make my own choices. Of course, I'm not free from the consequences of those choices. I've discovered that while God's love is unconditional, his promises are not. His promises are tied to our obedience.

Like a few million other people, I read *The Prayer of Jabez* this past year. Jabez prayed: "Oh, that you would bless me and enlarge my territory! Let your hand be with me, and keep me from harm so that I will be free from pain" (1 Chronicles 4:10). I began praying this for my children and myself daily. Of course, me being me, I was occasionally a bit bratty about the whole thing. One day, driving along in my car, I was crying out, more like Esau than Jabez, "Bless me—me, too, my father!" (Genesis 27:34). Unlike Jabez, who was "more honorable than his brothers" (1 Chronicles 4:9), Esau chose to sell his birthright to satisfy his stomach (Genesis 25:29–34). He was certainly free to make that choice; he liked that part. He wasn't so happy when the logical consequences of that choice came home to roost.

"Bless me! Bless me, too, Father," I cried, banging on the steering wheel. And God whispered, "My child, it would be a lot easier to bless you if you would be obedient." I stopped banging the steering wheel and looked up. Behold! The Dairy Queen! So I started thinking about the Dairy Queen. I imagined a couple scenarios.

Scenario #1: I'm driving along with my two little girls in the back seat. They are kicking and screaming at each other. Can I pull into the DQ at that moment and give them a reward? I mean, just as a responsible parent, is that a wise thing to do? Of course not.

Scenario #2: The kids and I have been out running errands all day, and they have been perfect little girls. They are singing praise songs and cuddling together in the back seat. Can I pull into the DQ? Yes! They have put themselves in a position where it is easy for me to bless them.

If you are looking for a place to stand, why not stand in a place where it is easy for God to bless you? A place of obedience? You may just discover the words of this psalm unfolding in your life:

> May he give you the desire of your heart
>   and make all your plans succeed.
> We will shout for joy when you are victorious
>   and will lift up our banners in the name of our God.
> May the Lord grant all your requests.

Stand at the Crossroads and Look:

1. Is it real to you that God loves you *exactly the same* whether you've having a good day or bad? Whether you make smart life choices or stupid ones? Why or why not?

2. How can that realization become life changing for you?

3. Are you the type of child who makes it easy for God to bless you? Or hard?

4. Right now, would you say you are standing in a place where it's easy for God to bless you? A place of obedience? Why or why not?

5. What changes is God calling you to make?

6. Write out a prayer expressing your desire to remain in a place where it's easy for God to bless you.

7. What key lesson did you glean from today's study?

Truths to Stand Upon:

- God's love is unconditional, but his promises are not.
- If you are looking for a place to stand, stand in a place where it is easy for God to bless you: a place of obedience.

Day Two

Standing on His Mercy and Grace

If you do not stand firm in your faith, you will not stand at all.
Isaiah 7:9

Yesterday, I shared about *The Prayer of Jabez* and the Dairy Queen. I didn't share the punch line. It wasn't until that moment that the truth hit me: I had spent twenty years asking God to bless my disobedience. And I was profoundly angry with him when he refused to do so. Even as I write these words, I have this terrible feeling in the pit of my stomach, this feeling that some people might misinterpret what I've shared on the pages of this book, that they might think I am somehow "advocating" divorce as an easy way out. Nothing could be farther from the truth. I can assure you there is nothing easy about divorce. I am not advocating my life choices; I am grieving them. However, I AM advocating God's mercy and grace, as it has become real to me that God's love is absolutely unconditional. I didn't deserve his love when he first reached down to rescue me from drug addiction, sexual promiscuity, and the host of other blatant sins that had enslaved me. And I don't deserve his love now, now that he has rescued me from my disastrous marriage and the bitterness, anger, and resentment that had enslaved me.

Several months ago, I heard the story of a woman who had made similar life choices. She, too, had married an Iranian man. Even though she had been a Christian from an early age, she chose to turn her back on Christ and to raise her children as Muslims. I don't know all the details of her life, but apparently she got what we both signed up for when we met charming Middle Eastern men: wealth, world travel, fancy cars, jewels, etc. (I never experienced those things because my husband's family lost everything in the Iranian Revolution.)

Her story was brought to my attention because she had returned to Christ and, even though her marriage had also ended in divorce, she was being hailed as a hero of the faith by Christian radio stations around the country. (And may I add, now that I'm more rational: AND RIGHTLY SO!)

At the time, however, I was LIVID. (I say this to my shame, sisters.) How dare she be featured on Christian radio when I had been unable to do any more Christian radio shows because of the shame of my divorce and the resulting outcry that had been raised against me. She was being bombarded with requests for speaking engagements. Meanwhile, nearly half of my speaking engagements had canceled. And most of them wouldn't even speak to me, wouldn't return my calls. I remember one church in particular. I have a file full of e-mails and letters from them, telling me how much they loved me and how God had used my books so powerfully in the life of their church. But when I was down, they canceled. I called the church in tears, asking if the pastor would just pray with me so I could get some peace, some closure. He refused. Only one church had their pastor call, explain their position,[1] and pray with me. The rest simply sent a letter, an e-mail, or left a phone message saying, "Don't bother to come." Okay, so here I am in the midst of this turmoil, and the church is throwing a parade for this other woman. How was this fair? *I was the one who stayed faithful to Christ. I was the one who stood firm.* This was an outrage. I was filled with indignation, bitterness, and resentment. I'd never even met this dear sister, and I wanted to strangle her!

One day, in the midst of my stewing, God paid me a visit in my kitchen. He spoke clearly, "My child, you are always with me and everything I have is yours." I began to cry. I immediately recognized it as Scripture, but I wasn't quite sure where it was from. I ran to my Bible and began searching. Do you know where the passage is found?

The story of the Prodigal Son. These are the words the Father had spoken to the *older brother*. I couldn't believe it. I had started out as the prodigal . . . and turned into the older brother. And do you want to know the sad truth? I was, in many ways, MORE lost in my role as older brother than I ever was as the prodigal. I was MORE lost sitting

---

[1]Their position was that everyone is saved by grace except divorced people who can only be saved by grounds. But even if they have grounds, they still can't teach anyone anything. Okay, okay, I'm being bratty here!

in a church pew, clutching my good doctrine, than I was rolling around in the back seat of a car with some teenage punk who forgot my name the next day. Yes, MORE lost as a Christian author and speaker than I was as a drug dealer.

How on earth can I say such a thing? Wasn't I on the way to heaven? Yes, but wasn't the older brother living in his father's house? But where was his HEART? His heart was far from his father. And my heart had become so filled with resentment that there was hardly any room left for God.

Over the past several weeks, I have been reading a Lenten devotional based on Henri Nouwen's book *The Return of the Prodigal Son.* It has spoken to the "older brother" within me in a very profound way. Let me share some of the truths I've jotted down in my journal:

> Resentment is probably one of the most pervasive evils of our time. It's something that is very real, very pernicious, and very, very destructive. Resentment is something that can settle itself in your heart and do a lot of damage. *It is precisely the pitfall of the faithful, obedient, hard-working people who do the right thing.*[2]
>
> Did you ever notice how lost you are when you are resentful? It's a very deep lostness. The younger son gets lost in a much more spectacular way. His wrongdoing is very clear-cut. He knows it and everybody else does, too. Because of it he can come back, and he can be forgiven. The problem with resentment is that it is not so clear-cut; it's not spectacular and it is not overt, and it can be covered by the appearance of a holy life. Resentment is so pernicious because it sits very deep in you, in your heart, in your bones, and in your flesh, and often you don't even know it is there. You think you're so good. But in fact you are lost in a very profound way.

No, my sisters, I am not advocating my choices. Certainly not advocating divorce. Just revealing for all the world how lost I had become, all the while sitting in a church pew, looking fairly spiritual. The prodigals in our midst KNOW they have nowhere to stand but upon the grace and mercy of our God. But I say to my fellow "older brothers" out there, we have nowhere else to stand either. We would

---

[2]"From Fear to Love: Lenten Reflections on the Parable of the Prodigal Son," excerpts from p. 13–14.

all be eternally lost if not for the grace and mercy of God. Good doctrine is good. Good behavior is even better. But we don't stand on doctrine or behavior. We stand on faith. The faith that says we are saved by grace, through faith and this not of ourselves, it is the gift of God (Ephesians 2:8–9). Remember: If we do not stand firm on our faith, we will not stand at all.

Stand at the Crossroads and Look:

1. Were you ever a prodigal? That is, engaged in blatant sin? Describe that place in your life and how God's grace and mercy met you there.

2. Can you identify at all with the older brother? How so?

3. Have you ever considered before that the older brother was, in some ways, MORE lost than the prodigal? What is your reaction to this possibility?

4. Is it possible that you are lost in some ways, even though you are a Christian?

5. Write out a prayer repenting of the older brother tendencies inside of you.

6. What key lesson did you glean from today's study?

Truths to Stand Upon:

- In many ways, the older brother was even more lost than the prodigal son.
- It's possible to be lost in a very profound way, even while sitting comfortably in a church pew, appearing fairly spiritual.

Day Three

Standing Firm on the Love of God

Therefore, my dear brothers, stand firm. Let nothing move you. Always give yourselves fully to the work of the Lord, because you know that your labor in the Lord is not in vain.

1 Corinthians 15:58

Chuck Swindoll once said (I know because I wrote it down in the front of my Bible): "We reap what we sow, forgiveness notwithstanding." I've been wrestling with this truth lately. What with *The Prayer of Jabez* and the DQ and that whole deal. And frankly, I started to get a little paranoid. I started meditating on passages like "Be sure that your sin will find you out" (Numbers 32:23). I started thinking, *I am such a pathetic loser! God is surely going to let me reap every last drop of the sin I have sown. I'm probably going to pay full-price for agreeing to this divorce. I can see it now: First, I'll lose my ministry, then I'll lose my house. Then since I'm living on the streets, I'll lose custody of my kids. When that happens, I'll lose my sanity and they'll lock me up forever. I'll lose my freedom. I'll lose everything that has ever mattered to me.*

I'm not exaggerating when I tell you that I nearly drove myself to the edge of a nervous breakdown with these fears. And let's face it, my fears were not entirely unfounded. Churches were canceling left and right; I had to put my house up for sale. Just as an extra bonus, I had the memory of my husband's repeated threats to kill me—or take my kids to Iran so I would never see them again—if I ever tried to leave him. And, oh yeah, did I mention that about this time Nikki's father suggested that since I stole his daughter, maybe someone might just steal one of mine? So I had some cause for paranoia, wouldn't you say? Besides, you've heard the horror stories about divorcées, haven't you? If not, call me and I'll fill you in. I have a friend who used to sit and tell me divorce horror stories all day long, in an attempt to scare me back into the marriage. Kinda creepy, now that I think about it, but she meant well.

Anyway, one day God brought 1 John 4:18 to my remembrance: "There is no fear in love. But perfect love drives out fear, because fear has to do with punishment. The [woman] who fears is not made perfect in love." Duh! Here's an excerpt from my prayer journal:

> I will rest securely in God's love only when I am *absolutely convinced* that he has my very best interests at heart. When I come to that place where I trust completely in God's love, I will have NOTHING to fear. No matter what happens. Even if God lets me reap the most dire consequences of my choices—even if I lose my house, lose my ministry, lose the high opinion of others, lose God only knows what else—even if I have to pay full price for every sin I have ever committed, it won't shake me. Because I'll know that even reaping consequences is not the same as punishment. It won't be because God hates me or is disgusted with me. It will be for my good. God loves me. That's settled. So chill out.

While it's hard for me to imagine what good could come out of losing everything that matters most to me, it's not my job to imagine. It's my job to stand firm and entrust myself to the one who judges justly. Since I've decided to open up my journal to you in this, our final week together, here's another excerpt:

> Interruptions are not disruptions on the way to holiness, but rather are places where you are being molded and formed into the person God calls you to be. You know you are living a grateful life when whatever happens is received as an invitation to deepen your heart, to strengthen your love and to broaden your hope. You are living a grateful life when something is taken away from you that you thought was so important and you find yourself willing to say, "Maybe I'm being invited to a deeper way of living."[3]

Lord, may we all learn to live grateful lives! As for getting all flipped out because of what other people thought about me (frankly,

---

[3]Nouwen, p. 8.

this has been the hardest part!), here's some food for thought that God brought to my attention:

At age 20, we worry about what other people think about us.
At age 40, we don't care what other people think about us.
At age 60, we realize people weren't really thinking that much about us!

And besides, if other people want to set themselves up as judge and jury over your life, that's their problem, not yours. Romans 14:4 says, "Who are you to judge someone else's servant? To his own master he stands or falls. And he will stand, for the Lord is able to make him stand." Second Corinthians 1:21–22 reiterates: "Now it is God who makes both us and you stand firm in Christ. He anointed us, set his seal of ownership on us, and put his Spirit in our hearts as a deposit, guaranteeing what is to come."

So wait a minute here. We've spent ten weeks learning how to stand firm, and at the eleventh hour, we realize even THAT—even our ability to stand firm—is a gift of God. What do we have that he did not freely give us? Wow. What an awesome God. What unfathomable love!

Therefore, my dear sisters (because of that unfathomable love which he has freely given us in Christ), stand firm. Let nothing move you. Always give yourselves fully to the work of the Lord, because you know that your labor in the Lord is not in vain.

Stand at the Crossroads and Look:

1. Does the fact that "we reap what we sow, forgiveness notwithstanding" make you a little paranoid? Why or why not?

2. Do you truly believe that even if you were to end up reaping the full consequences of every stupid choice, it wouldn't shake your confidence in God's love and care for you?

3. Have you come to the place where you are absolutely convinced that God always has your very best interests at heart?

4. Are you living a grateful life?

5. Write out a prayer expressing your confidence in God's love and care for you.

6. What key lesson did you glean from today's study?

Truths to Stand Upon:

- We reap what we sow, forgiveness notwithstanding.
- Reaping consequences is not the same as punishment. If God allows us to reap what we sow, it is an expression of his love for us.
- We will rest securely in God's love only when we are absolutely convinced that he has our best interests at heart.

Day Four

Stand Your Ground

We are not of those who shrink back and are destroyed, but of those who believe and are saved.

Hebrews 10:39

It had been another one of "those days." Finally, in absolute exhaustion and despair, I sat at the kitchen table, put my head down, and starting sobbing. My children came over, put their arms around me, and prayed for God to "help Mommy" because Mommy clearly needed all the help she could get. When they had finished praying, Leah, then age ten, looked at me solemnly and said, "I think I know why all this is happening to you." "Really," I replied. "Tell me about it." She explained, "Well, I think it's because you are a *first-generation Christian.*"

I looked up at her. For once, at a loss for words. I could tell this was something she had been giving much thought to. "What do you mean?"

"Think about it, Mom. No one in your family has ever been a Christian. You're the only one. Satan knows that if he can beat you, then it will be easy to steal us away, then what chance will our family have? You have to be strong for all of us. Don't let him beat you."

Unbelievable. My ten year old had grabbed hold of a truth that eludes most adult Christians: Lions always target the most vulnerable animal in the pack—and that's usually the youngest. Scripture plainly tells us, "Your enemy the devil prowls around like a roaring lion looking for someone to devour" (1 Peter 5:8). If you are a first-generation Christian, don't be surprised that standing firm is a much tougher assignment for you than for the person next to you, whose mother and grandmother and great-grandmother were Christians. YOU are a primary target for attack, not them. It's not your imagination. You're not going crazy. Your life IS much more difficult.

When I share this story in person, I look around and can spot the first-generation Christians with ease. They are weeping, and there's a light bulb that has just turned on over their heads. I also share a story about another woman who chose to stand firm in the face of seemingly insurmountable obstacles.[4] As the Civil War was drawing to a close, the Confederate army moved from town to town, warning people to make way for the advancing Union army. One day they happened upon a small Virginia farmhouse and told the family they had to leave. But the woman explained, "I am a widow with three small children. I have nowhere else to go." The soldiers tried to convince her to leave, tried to impress upon her the gravity of her situation. "There is an ARMY coming against you. Don't you understand?" they exclaimed. "This is my home," she replied with quiet confidence. "God has promised to protect us. This is where we'll stay."

The Union army did sweep through Virginia that night. And they burned and pillaged everything in their path. The next morning, in the midst of the rubble and the ashes, one house stood. It was the house of that widow. Curious, the Confederate soldiers returned to ask, "Who were all those men guarding your house last night?"

Well, we know who they were! God himself sent an army of angels. First, God *asked* her to stand firm. Then he *enabled* her to stand firm. Repeat: God ASKED her to stand firm and the minute she took a step of faith, he sent down help from heaven to ENABLE her to stand firm. Amazing. It will be the same for you. In case you are wondering how I know that story, it's because I am friends with her great, great, great, great, great, great, great granddaughter, Joy Morse. The true story of that widow's incredible faith has been passed down, now to the ninth generation of her descendants.

Sometimes people will come up to me and apologize for not having a testimony. I tell them "testimony" is just a polite way of saying you've made a mess of your life. If that widow's story had not been passed down, no doubt her descendants would be standing around apologizing for their lack of testimony. The simple fact is, no family moves from the kingdom of darkness into the kingdom of his blessed

---

[4]I shared this story previously in *Walking in Total God-Confidence*, but I think it warrants retelling.

light without someone, somewhere paying a high price. Maybe your mother, your grandmother, your great-grandmother paid that price for you and you just don't know about it. You should never apologize for receiving the greatest gift any parent can give her children: the gift of a godly inheritance. But don't squander it either. Don't become an "older brother" type Christian. One who lives in the Father's house but is far from expressing the Father's heart of compassion. Be determined to pass onto your children a vibrant, living faith in our merciful God.

My sisters, if you have been looking for a reason to stand firm, look no further. Look to your children. To your grandchildren and all who will come after you. You must do what's right and best for your children, even if it means standing against a whole army of public opinion. And it will surely mean standing against the onslaught of garbage our culture is spewing forth. If you don't think your family is under attack, turn on the television.

The Psalmist wrote, "Though an army besiege me, my heart will not fear; though war break out against me, even then will I be confident" (Psalm 27:3). Put another way, even then I will choose to stand firm. There's a war being waged for our families. The eternal destiny of many generations to come are at stake. The writer of Hebrews declared, "We are not of those who shrink back and are destroyed, but of those who believe and are saved" (Hebrews 10:39). May it be said of you that you did not shrink back, not even in the face of overwhelming obstacles, but that you chose to continue believing God, that you chose to stand firm.

Stand at the Crossroads and Look:

1. Are you a first-generation Christian? What have been the ramifications of that for you? For your children?

2. Have you inherited a godly dynasty? Do you know anything you can share about those who paved the way, that you might inherit a blessing? If not, why not do some investigating?

3. Write out a prayer thanking God for his saving grace toward your family.

4. What key lesson did you glean from today's study?

Truths to Stand Upon:

- If you are a first-generation Christian, don't be surprised to discover that standing firm is a far greater challenge for you. You are a prime target for the enemy.
- No family moves from the kingdom of darkness into the kingdom of his blessed light without someone paying a high price.

Day Five

Standing Firm in Fear and Trembling

When I came to you, brothers, I did not come with eloquence or superior wisdom as I proclaimed to you the testimony about God. For I resolved to know nothing while I was with you except Jesus Christ and him crucified. I came to you in weakness and fear, and with much trembling. My message and my preaching were not with wise and persuasive words, but with a demonstration of the Spirit's power, so that your faith might not rest on men's wisdom, but on God's power.

1 Corinthians 2:1–5

It started with a transposed verse. I was doing a presentation on my previous book *Living in Absolute Freedom*, when I referenced 1 Corinthians 4:2. It's my favorite teaching, about "living our lives before an Audience of One." Unfortunately, since I love teaching it so much, God continually gives me opportunities to practice living it myself. Uh-oh! Anyway, one of the women turned to 1 Corinthians 2:4 instead. She came up afterward and told me she had looked up the wrong verse. *So what?* I thought to myself. *Why are you telling me this?* She sensed that I was puzzled and explained, "I think you should look it up. But backtrack to verse 1. It sums up exactly what has happened here this weekend." Okay, here's the verse:

When I came to you, brothers, I did not come with eloquence or superior wisdom as I proclaimed to you the testimony about God. For I resolved to know nothing while I was with you except Jesus Christ and him crucified. I came to you in weakness and fear, and with much trembling. My message and my preaching were not with wise and persuasive words, but with a demonstration of the Spirit's power, so that your faith might not rest on men's wisdom, but on God's power.

A couple hours ago when I was goofing off on the Internet instead of finishing this one last page (which I've been procrastinating over for an entire week), I noticed that the award for the Pulitzer Prize in Literature had just been announced. I didn't even look to see if I had won. I've read enough brilliant authors to know I'm not one of them. As for superior wisdom, I've got zilch. I have a friend, around my age, who has a continual lineup of women begging her to "mentor" and "disciple" them. Gotta fess up here, friends: No one has ever asked to be my protégé. Nope. No brilliance. No eloquence. No superior wisdom. I have no magic formula to offer. No program to implement. I only know one thing: Jesus came to save sinners, and I sure am a sinner in need of saving. And I didn't just need his saving grace twenty years ago; I needed it all day today. Wait a minute, I know one other thing: If God could save me, no one is beyond his reach.

As I turn this now-finished book over to my editor, I do so "in weakness and fear, and with much trembling." And I think that's a healthy place to be. I know that if the Spirit of God does not demonstrate his power through its pages, the whole endeavor has been in vain. It has just been another tree-killing expedition. I don't want you to finish this book and declare, "Wow, that Donna is one wise woman. She's a real spiritual giant; I could never be like her." Of course, now that I've bared my soul, there's not much chance of that happening! I often tell my audiences that "God wants to use you, not in spite of your brokenness, but because of it." Well, now's my chance to find out if I really believe what I teach. My prayer is that you will walk away, strengthened in your faith, not because you gleaned words of wisdom from me, but that you will walk away, strengthened in your faith, because God himself has worked powerfully in your life these past ten weeks. I am trusting God to work, not in spite of my brokenness but because of it.

Jamie Owens-Collins recently shared with me her philosophy of ministry; I've adopted it as my own. She said she envisions herself as a servant working at a dinner party. You know, the kind where the staff walk around carrying trays filled with scrumptious food. Jamie pointed out that the host decides what gets put on the tray; the guests decide what they want to take off. There's plenty of food for the taking, but it's not the servant's job to force-feed anyone. The invited guests get to pick and choose. Our job, as servants of the King, is to simply hold up the tray. To offer whatever morsels of truth God has entrusted to us, to whoever decides to show up for the party.

That's what I've done. I've been holding the tray, and I have watched in amazement as God has reached down to place food on it. When I write, I write quickly! My fingers literally fly over the keyboard, well in excess of one hundred words per minute. My fingers are moving faster than my brain. Half the time, I don't even know what I'm writing. I can't even stop to read it because more is coming. And I feel this urgency to press forward. To keep typing. I almost never stop to think "Gee, what should I write about next? Or how can I put this?"

I wrote the majority of *Becoming a Vessel God Can Use* in four days; *Living in Absolute Freedom* took less than two weeks; *Walking in Total God-Confidence* and this book took a bit more. But not much. People are astonished when they hear that, especially if they've done any writing themselves. But if we think about my role as the tray holder, it makes perfect sense. I didn't choose the menu, and I didn't cook the food. That's the hard work, the time-consuming part. I just stood there while it was placed on the tray.

And that doesn't take very long at all. That's why I take no credit when people share the powerful way God uses my books in their lives. While I'm happy to extend their compliments to the chef, it never even crosses my mind that I might BE the chef. Believe me, I can't cook. I'm just holding the tray, friends. And I'm overwhelmed with gratefulness that the chef keeps someone like me on staff.

I'm living proof that God is looking for willing servants, not perfect servants. So pick up a tray and stand firm. God himself will place morsels on the tray that you might share with those who are hungering for his truth.

How is it possible that we have come to the end of another ten-week journey together? And what shall I leave you with? I leave you with a prayer:

> I pray also that the eyes of your heart may be enlightened in order that you may know the hope to which he has called you, the riches of his glorious inheritance in the saints, and his incomparably great power for us who believe. (Ephesians 1:18–19)

Stand at the Crossroads and Look:

1. Take some time to reflect upon the most significant lessons you've learned over the past ten weeks.

2. Write out a prayer to God thanking him for enabling you to stand firm.

3. What key lesson did you glean from today's study?

4. Write out This Week's Verse from memory.

Truths to Stand Upon:

- Our job, as servants of the King, is to simply hold up the tray, to offer whatever morsels of truth God has entrusted to us to whoever decides to show up for the party.
- It's not the servant's job to force-feed the guests.
- God is looking for willing servants, not perfect servants.

Weekly Review:

Take a few moments to fill in the ten actions and attitudes required to Stand Firm. Look in the back of the book if you need help.

S _____ God first

S _____ God's perspective

S _____ your spiritual hunger

S _____ the love God has for you

S _____ yourself against the attacks of the enemy

S _____ truth to yourself and others

S _____ the tide of mediocrity

S _____ like a saint

S _____ wholeheartedly

S _____ firm until the end

Steps to Freedom

1. *Know that God loves you.* "For God so loved the world that he gave his one and only Son, that whoever believes in him shall not perish but have eternal life." (John 3:16)
2. *Acknowledge your sin.* "For all have sinned and fall short of the glory of God." (Romans 3:23)
3. *Turn from sin.* "Therefore do not let sin reign in your mortal body so that you obey its evil desires. Do not offer the parts of your body to sin, as instruments of wickedness, but rather offer yourselves to God." (Romans 6:12–13)
4. *Accept that Jesus is the only way.* "I am the way and the truth and the life. No one comes to the Father except through me." (John 14:6) "Salvation is found in no one else, for there is no other name under heaven given to men by which we must be saved." (Acts 4:12)
5. *Realize that Jesus paid the penalty for your sins.* "But he was pierced for our transgressions, he was crushed for our iniquities; the punishment that brought us peace was upon him, and by his wounds we are healed. We all, like sheep, have gone astray, each of us has turned to his own way; and the Lord has laid on him the iniquity of us all." (Isaiah 53:5–6)
6. *Receive Jesus as Savior.* "Here I am! I stand at the door and knock. If anyone hears my voice and opens the door, I will come in and eat with him, and he with me." (Revelation 3:20) "Yet to all who received him, to those who believed in his name, he gave the right to become children of God." (John 1:12)

A Note to Leaders

Dear Bible Study Leaders:

I want to thank you for choosing *Standing Firm*, not just for your own use, but to share with the women God has entrusted to your care. It's a great honor to know that, among all the excellent Bible study materials available, you consider my book worthwhile.

I pray that this journey will lead you into a deeper love relationship with God and into closer fellowship with the women who participate. I realize that many people like to sit down and tackle one book in one sitting, rather than playing by my one-day-at-a-time rule. In the past, I've winked at this misbehavior, but in the case of *Standing Firm*, I think you should strongly encourage the women *not* to read ahead. They will require eight weeks of prayerful preparation to handle the information contained in Week Nine.

As with my previous studies, I would encourage you to use visuals whenever possible. Do all you can to bring the study to life, and it will bring life to those who participate. Speaking of participants, I'm including a Participant Profile worksheet. Please make photocopies of it to use with your class. During your first meeting, ask each person to complete the questionnaire. Allow plenty of time for this exercise. The insight you will gain will be extremely valuable as you seek to meet the needs of each woman. Once everyone has finished, spend time discussing their responses *but don't call on anyone*. People do not like to be "put on the spot," so let them know from the beginning that your policy is to encourage—but not require—participation in the discussion.

Make it a point to contact each woman on a regular basis *outside* the classroom environment. It could be a phone call, a note card, or a trip to the park together. The key is to demonstrate a personal interest in their spiritual growth and well-being. The profile sheets will give you a good place to start in understanding each woman's needs and initiating conversation.

The one exception to the "no putting people on the spot" rule is the memory verse cards, which you'll find at the back of the book. Each week, at the very beginning of class, ask each woman to recite her verse from memory. Do it in a spirit of fun and out of a desire to "spur one another on toward love and good deeds." Be sensitive and avoid embarrassing anyone. Nevertheless, when the women come to understand that they will be expected to recite their verse, almost all will rise to the occasion and put in the extra effort required.

If women will carry their memory verse cards with them wherever they go, there is absolutely no reason why they can't memorize one verse per week. All three of my previous books contain helpful suggestions on Scripture memory; I haven't repeated that information here, but you can readily put your hands on it. Using these techniques, anyone can learn to memorize Scripture effectively. I have included some new ideas on promoting Scripture memory in Week Six, Day One.

Along with each week's memory verse, I have also included a few key thoughts to summarize the lesson. These do not have to be memorized but will help the women get the most out of the study.

Finally, you'll notice that there is a Weekly Review Test included each week. It's always the same test, but hopefully the women will get better and better scores. Again, make it a point to take the test as a group every week by reciting in unison the ten attitudes and actions required for Standing Firm.

When your group successfully completes the study, I would love nothing more than to receive a photograph of all you beautiful ladies. I like to put these on the wall of my home office, to prevent me from "growing weary in well-doing." I really cherish every letter I receive, although I must admit I'm not that great about writing back. Just know in advance, you'll do the heart of this princess some good!

His vessel,
Donna Partow
P.O. Box 842
Payson, AZ 85541
donnapartow@cybertrails.com

Participant Profile Sheet

Name: _____ Phone: _____

Address: _____

_____

_____

Reason for enrolling in this class: _____

_____

_____

_____

_____

What is the most pressing problem/challenge in your life right now?

_____

_____

_____

How can this class (and your fellow classmates) help you cope more effectively?

_____

_____

_____

_____

How do you want your life to be different at the end of this study?

_____

_____

_____

_____

What are some specific habits you want to improve?

_____

_____

_____

_____

_____

List five things you expect from a women's Bible study. (Indicate things you like/dislike.)

1. _____

2. _____

3. _____

4. _____

5. _____

Thinking back on prior experiences with Bible studies, what motivated you to finish a class? What might cause you to drop out of a class?

_____

_____

_____

_____

How can your leader help you to get the most out of this class?

_____

_____

_____

_____

_____

ARE YOU READY TO BE CHANGED?

The Life Lessons to Be Learned From the Bible's Gardens

Jane Rubietta is holding open a gate to the two most important gardens in the Bible—Eden and Gethsemane—allowing you take an the ultimate soul-journey. Masterfully weaving together the analogy of our souls as gardens with God as our caretaker, she provides Scripture passages and special insight into both Eden and Gethsemane, challenging us to experience personal growth and new life.

Between Two Gardens
by Jane Rubietta

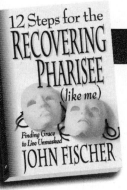

Who Are We to Judge?

Jesus defined truth in such a way as to leave no one righteous—not one. We cannot be made right before God by being "better" than anyone else. Instead, by recognizing and laying aside the Pharisee in all of us, we can learn to embrace the grace, gratitude, and joy of the spirit-filled life.

12 Steps for the Recovering Pharisee
by John Fischer

◊BETHANYHOUSE

11400 Hampshire Ave S.
Minneapolis, MN 55438
800-328-6109
www.bethanyhouse.com

Week 4: Isaiah 54:9–10

"So now I have sworn not to be angry with you. . . .
Though the mountains be shaken
     and the hills be removed,
yet my unfailing love for you will not be shaken
     nor my covenant of peace be removed,"
says the Lord, who has compassion on you.
(NIV)

Standing Firm, Donna Partow

Week 1: Hebrews 11:6

But without faith it is impossible to please Him, for he who comes to God must believe that He is, and that He is a rewarder of those who diligently seek Him. (NKJV)

Standing Firm, Donna Partow

Week 5: 1 Peter 5:8–9

Be self-controlled and alert. Your enemy the devil prowls around like a roaring lion looking for someone to devour. Resist him, standing firm in the faith, because you know that your brothers throughout the world are undergoing the same kind of sufferings. (NIV)

Standing Firm, Donna Partow

Week 2: Jeremiah 33:3

Call to me and I will answer you and tell you great and unsearchable things that you do not know. (NIV)

Standing Firm, Donna Partow

Week 6: John 17:15–17

"My prayer is not that you take them out of the world but that you protect them from the evil one. They are not of the world, even as I am not of it. Sanctify them by the truth; your word is truth." (NIV)

Standing Firm, Donna Partow

Week 3: Jeremiah 15:16

Your words are what sustain me; they are food to my hungry soul. They bring joy to my sorrowing heart and delight me. How proud I am to bear your name, O Lord. (TLB)

Standing Firm, Donna Partow

Week 4: Savor the Love God Has for You

- Stand firm on what you know to be true, whether or not anyone else believes in you.
- God knows the truth about your circumstances; he believes in you.
- If you run to your brothers and sisters in Christ, rather than seeking God first, you will remain a desolate woman.
- When we draw near to God, we are automatically nearer to those who are near to the heart of God.
- God wants us to have an intimate conversation with you, but he won't do it in the midst of chaos.

Week 1: Seek God First

- Standing firm means living the life God has handed you, without explanation, without apology.
- We often learn how to stand firm only after mastering the art of stumbling.
- Sometimes we are overwhelmed by forces outside of our control.
- We become "caged in" by our own foolish choices, but God wants us to regain our freedom.
- We need to strengthen our spiritual hearts through daily exercise.
- God has promised to guide us always, even through a sun-scorched land.

Week 5: Strengthen Yourself Against the Attacks of the Enemy

- We should see Satan for the "roaring lion" he is: don't run. Stand firm
- Doubting the goodness of God leads to rebellion; resting in the goodness of God leads to obedience.
- We are beloved children of a gracious King.
- Since a stronghold is fabricated with lies, the only way to demolish it is with truth.
- The primary weapons of our warfare are: the Word of God and prayer.
- The most effective prayers we can offer on behalf of our loved ones are those taken directly from the pages of Scripture.

Week 2: Sustain God's Perspective

- When we call upon God, he will answer us.
- If we want God's perspective, we should ask God.
- When we keep the phone line open to God, he will prosper and not harm us.
- God wants our obedience, not our game plan.
- It's possible that God wants to give you something greater than healing: a whole new life.
- Having our heart in the right place is not enough. We must sustain God's perspective, as well.

Week 6: Speak Truth to Yourself and Others

- Our mind will find whatever we tell it to look for, whether positive or negative.
- Many of us are caught in downward emotional spirals because we are constantly looking for—and finding—what's right with the world, rather than what's wrong with it.
- Sharing a truth forces you to process the information in such a way that it goes into a deeper part of your brain. When you apply it to a specific situation, it is even more firmly planted in your mind.
- We must help our sisters find rest and "take possession" of all that God has for them. Will you speak the truth to them?
- There's a world filled with hurting people. Will

Week 3: Satisfy Your Spiritual Hunger

- We live within self-imposed boundaries because we haven't bothered to test the limits.
- Crash through your self-imposed boundaries and feast on what your soul is really hungering for:
- As you feed your spirit a healthy diet, your cravings for mental junk food will subside.
- If you would truly satisfy your spiritual hunger, then you must feast on the *whole counsel* of God.

Week 8: Habakkuk 3:17–18

Though the fig tree does not bud
    and there are no grapes on the vines,
though the olive crop fails
    and the fields produce no food
though there are no sheep in the pen
    and no cattle in the stalls,
yet I will rejoice in the Lord
    I will be joyful in God my Savior. (NIV)

Standing Firm, Donna Partow

Standing Firm

- **SEEK** God first
- **SUSTAIN** God's perspective
- **SATISFY** your spiritual hunger
- **SAVOR** the love God has for you
- **STRENGTHEN** yourself against the attacks of the enemy
- **SPEAK** truth to yourself and others
- **STEM** the time of mediocrity
- **SUFFER** like a saint
- **SERVE** wholeheartedly
- **STAND** firm until the end

Standing Firm, Donna Partow

Week 9: Jeremiah 15:19

Therefore, thus says the Lord,
"If you return, then I will restore you—
Before Me you will stand;
And if you extract the precious from the worthless
You will become My spokesman." (NASB)

Standing Firm, Donna Partow

Week 10: Psalm 20:7–8

Some trust in chariots and some in horses,
    but we trust in the name of the LORD our God.
They are brought to their knees and fall,
    but we rise up and stand firm. (NIV)

Standing Firm, Donna Partow

Week 7: John 14:6

Jesus answered, "I am the way and the truth and the life. No one comes to the Father except through me." (NIV)

Standing Firm, Donna Partow

Week 8: Suffer Like a Saint

- If God loves us and is in charge of what happens in the world, then we must receive EVERY-THING that comes our way as having first been filtered through the hands of a loving God.
- Rather than focusing on how someone has hurt you, consider how you might minister healing to her.
- God has compassion on our human frailties.
- Suffering that is ordained by God always has a purpose, for God's glory and our own good.
- Jesus wants to heal us and "stop the bleeding."

Week 9: Serve Wholeheartedly

- The world breaks everyone, and afterward many are strong at the broken places.
- For those struggling with low self-esteem, we must "bestow on them a crown of beauty."
- We need to "proclaim freedom for the captives," of loneliness.
- Christ is calling us "to comfort all who mourn and provide for those who grieve in Zion."
- We must extend grace and mercy to the prodigal.
- If we would serve wholeheartedly, we must begin by forgiving ourselves and others.

Week 10: Stand Firm Until the End

- God's love is unconditional, but his promises are not.
- Stand in a place where it is easy for God to bless you: a place of obedience.
- It's possible to be lost even while sitting comfortably in a church pew.
- We reap what we sow, forgiveness notwithstanding.
- We will rest securely in God's love when we are convinced he has our best interests at heart.
- If you are a first-generation Christian, you are a prime target for the enemy.

Week 7: Stem the Tide of Mediocrity

- If we want to touch our world we must offer real solutions for real people in the real world.
- The real Gospel has been bringing people into the Kingdom for 2,000 years; there's no need to switch now.
- It's *how* you live that matters.
- Beware the temptation to live minute wise and hour foolish.
- If we would stem the tide of mediocrity, we must use our minutes wisely.
- Invite others to spur you on in your spiritual growth.